A FORGOTTEN WORLD

Lessons From the Great Depression

By

A. H. Blegen

ISBN: 1-4107-5599-1 (e-book)
ISBN: 1-4107-5598-3 (Paperback)

This book is printed on acid free paper.

1stBooks – rev. 6/27/03

CONTENTS

ACKNOWLEDGMENTS

Special thanks to Gus Heinold and Gordon Anderson who provided early critiques of the manuscript and to Brad Blegen and Kathleen Huntley for careful reading at important junctures.

Also, thanks to editor, Kathleen Stoehr, of Chemistry Creative, for valuable assistance and editing on this book.

OTHER BOOKS BY A.H. BLEGEN

A Place With Two Bells (a novel)

Records Management Step-by-Step

♦INTRODUCTION♦

As I begin this book I'm celebrating (what a misnomer) my seventy-ninth birthday. Is today's world just older than when I was eight or eighteen or twenty-eight or is it a different world? I'll take you back to my world of those early years, the 1930s and World War II. Then I'll compare it to today's world. I'll labor diligently, not always successfully, to refrain from conclusions, just my experiences and opinions. You be the judge.

Before we begin this journey there are some facts you should know about me, not the routine biographical type, but personality facts. I abhor hypocrisy. Hypocrites are the bane of civilized discourse. No solutions to problems can be achieved when hypocrisy prevails.

Logic should be the device we use to make decisions. Emotions are important, but they exist for us to feel sorrow or experience happiness, not dictate our choices. If we don't plan our future logically, if we don't make decisions logically, there is no future for this country.

I love Billie Holiday. For those who never heard her, she was the greatest female jazz singer to ever live. Born in 1915, she died in 1959. No one translated life into song like Billie Holiday. I believe one's taste in music tells a lot about that person. But more about Holiday later.

Baseball is my favorite sport. It's a thinking person's game, one that requires high levels of timing, coordination and dexterity of its players. The thrill, in the late innings, of a one to nothing game is unparalleled. And it doesn't matter where it's played. Amateur town ball with fifty spectators cheering for thirty- or forty-year-old players is equally exciting as fifty thousand fans at a major league game.

So how is today's world different from the world of my youth? I'll review it for you in a myriad of areas: childhood, growing up (the teen years), education, family, work, music, recreation, government, safety, patriotism and, lastly, our future. At the end of each chapter I will repeat the question, "Are there lessons to be learned from the Great Depression days?" Then I'll summarize a point or two from that chapter. These will be opinions, not statistics. Statistics, after all, can be shaped and bent to reflect any opinion. There is no large bibliography, no long list of annotated notes in this book, just my meditations on these two periods in our history.

For readers of my age group this book is written to remember, nostalgically, the "old days" and how life has changed today. For young readers it's an opportunity to learn about life during the Great Depression, the 1930s, and the World War II years, the years of their parent's or grandparent's youth. Come along with me, agree or disagree, but be honest in how you judge my reflections of *A Forgotten World*.

I admit to an event that energized me for this task. It was a book written by Farah Jasmine Griffin titled *If You Can't be Free, be a Mystery,* a search for an understanding of Billie Holiday. Ms. Griffin was not satisfied with the bibliography-oriented approach to existing books about this artist. She wanted to capture the spirit and passion in this artist's life, to explore the meaning it had for contemporary black women, especially black artists, so they might appreciate and better understand their struggles. It's a beautiful book written to teach all of us not to be misled by the myths, repeated ad infinitum, that frequently portray public entertainers inaccurately.

I have a similar objective for readers of *A Forgotten World*. Don't be misled by the myths that more money in our pockets, and more freedom to do whatever feels good, is progress. The world has changed, radically, drastically, in the past few decades. Let us look at these changes and ask ourselves, "Is this better? Or is it a myth?"

This is not a book about liberalism or conservatism, Democrats or Republicans, progressives or reactionaries. It's a book about who we were fifty to seventy-five years ago and what we are today. Which do you want for your future? Can we understand the changes? Have we had "progress" that leads us somewhere or nowhere?

Henry David Thoreau, renowned naturalist and author, in his conclusion to his 1845 book, *Walden,* wrote, "If you have built castles in the air, your work need not be lost; that is where they should be. Now put the foundations under them."

This country is young in the annals of countries. We have built our castles but how strong and trustworthy are the foundations?

Why do I have credibility to write a book comparing the 1930s and early 1940s with the first decade of the Twenty-first Century? Because I have lived in both periods, have observed and experienced many events and changes of fortune in seventy-nine years, and have the passion to write about it. I believe our country needs information and advice from people who have a long-range perspective versus a "quick fix" mentality. The periods deserve comparison to belie the myth that history teaches us nothing and technological advancements solve all our problems. In Thucydides' *History of the Peloponnesian War* (Jowett's translation), Pericles, a leading statesman of Athens, is quoted in 431 B.C., "We alone regard a man who takes no interest in public affairs, not as a harmless, but as a useless character; and if few of us are originators, we are all sound judges of a policy. The great impediment to action is, in our opinion, not discussion, but the want of that knowledge which is gained by discussion preparatory to action."

Amen!

♦ Chapter One: **CHILDHOOD**

My mother died in childbirth, giving birth to me, the ultimate sacrifice a mother can make for a child. I didn't understand this until I was older and looking back at her life.

In the decade before her marriage to my father in 1922, she taught school in places like Adams and Heil, Stebbins and Odessa, and Bentley and Brisbane, all in North Dakota. These towns have either disappeared from current maps or, literally, dried up and blew away in the depression days of the 1930s. But the schools weren't in the towns. They were in the country, in the middle of nowhere, one-room affairs, often with six students all in different grades. My mother boarded each year with a farm family of one of her students and often, in the winter, rode horseback to school, the only mode of transportation when the snows were deep. I can only imagine the isolated, solitary life this presented a young woman.

But I was lucky after my birth in 1924. My father was already caring for two aged parents on a remote farm in central North Dakota. The concept of nursing or retirement homes had not been invented at that time. Families cared for their own until death intervened. My father did not feel capable of adding a baby to his responsibilities so an aunt in Minneapolis took me and raised me as her son. I could not have had a more wise, loving mother. My aunt's husband, my uncle, died when I was one-year old but my aunt had a son and two

1

daughters. The daughters became like sisters to me, the son, twenty-years older, like my father. I always called my aunt "mother" but to avoid confusion in this book she will henceforth be called stepmother.

At the age of three my stepmother entered me in Sunday School (called the "Cradle Roll" at that time) at Central Lutheran Church in downtown Minneapolis. She was active in church affairs, cooking and baking to provide lunches and dinners for church activities. She took me everywhere. Baby sitters were a rarity in the 1930s. Before the age of five I spent long hours in the church coloring in a book or looking at pictures. I ate everything the kindly ladies in the kitchen gave me, on the sly, as they prepared meals for the church. They would compete with each other to give me the sweetest cookie just out of the oven or the most flavorful scoop of ice cream and say, "Isn't he cute? Look at that long blonde hair and how quietly he sits." Luckily my stepmother didn't take me to church every day or I would have grown to monstrous proportions. And here we come to the first contrast between our world today and the world of the late twenties and thirties, essentially the Great Depression years. My stepmother brought me to church and told me to sit quietly, sometimes for hours, and speak only when spoken to. That's how I behaved. I knew no other behavior. Contrast that with today's children who, as a group, can't sit quietly for more than a few minutes, tell their parents what they want to eat, where they want to eat it, what they want to wear, from what store and what they will watch on television and how long.

As I grew older I had only one baseball, one football and one basketball. I kept sewing them up until they disintegrated. They were leather in those days, not some imitation material. We didn't need a coach to call us together for an organized practice. Each neighborhood had numerous empty lots and we turned those into playfields. My stepmother called me for lunch and dinner but the rest of my day was spent playing sports. As a result I became well coordinated in athletics and enjoyed amateur softball, basketball, tennis and golf well into my fifties and sixties.

Journey to any manicured, pristine, well-equipped local playfield today and you will find it deserted except for a few hours in the late afternoon when a coach calls some boys and girls together for a one-hour practice, watched intensely by the parents, but probably disliked by the young boys and girls who can't possibly attain any skill level under those circumstances.

That is the reason we have major league baseball players today who have skipped the fundamentals of baseball while they advanced from twice-a-week, little league practice to high school and, perhaps, some college experience. After a year or two in a minor league they show up on one of thirty major league teams unskilled in many areas.

Yes, the players are stronger and bigger now but catchers still stab for an errant pitch with their glove instead of shifting their body, few outfielders can turn their back at the crack of a bat and run down a fly ball and a pitcher who works more than six innings is considered an iron man. In the thirties, in the high minor leagues, there were pitchers who frequently pitched doubleheaders on a Sunday afternoon. That's eighteen innings!

I walked to school. There were no school buses in the city of Minneapolis except to serve handicapped children. It was often a mile in twenty-below-zero weather, much longer if you lived in the country. It was an early lesson that life contained hardships. Busing today is not about convenience. It's more about tolerating an unpleasant ride of up to an hour twice a day unless the student gets a ride from indulging parents or becomes a teenager with a driver's license.

In school I sat quietly, never with a hat on my head, and learned the multiplication tables, to add and subtract from memory, do division on paper and all without an adding machine, much less a computer. Today? Well, I can't count the times I've watched an eighteen-year-old store clerk struggle to make change because they have never absorbed any arithmetic in their heads.

The schools didn't spend any time teaching seven-year-olds about diversity and sex. Most young people came from families hard hit by the depression and required no education in sympathizing with other young people also experiencing hardships. In Minneapolis, on my low to medium class neighborhood block, we had three minority families whose children were integrated with the other children in the block, went to school with them and played with them from morning to night. Norwegian, Polish or black, we all got along.

I know minorities were discriminated against in Minneapolis in restaurants, hotels and some entertainment venues but, up North at least, the integration was superior to the perceptions that have prevailed these many years. I believe the Midwest was fortunate in not having numerous ethnic enclaves that often foster jealousy and conflict between groups.

In grade school I was "given time to be a child" as opposed to today's young people bombarded with sex and diversity when they are incapable of even spelling the words. Time is needed at this age to develop naturally and orderly (call it slowly, if you wish) before more serious problems are encountered.

We rush our children today and they develop all types of syndromes and dependence on drugs before they learn to act responsibly. This tragedy will haunt us forever.

As we progressed into our early teens we became more independent but still respectful to adults and thankful for ordinary food and adequate clothing. As a seven-year-old in 1931 I scrubbed the kitchen floor and the outside stairway on my hands and knees for my stepmother for an allowance of ten cents a week. As a fifteen-year-old I sorted out rotten potatoes in a grocery store for fifteen cents an hour. I know inflation has made those statistics irrelevant but fifteen cents an hour was not big money even in 1939.

I had other responsibilities before I reached my teen years. There were no refrigerators but we had an icebox. An icebox cooled food by holding chunks of ice in an upper compartment. As the ice melted the water ran down a tube into a pan on the floor. It was my job to empty the pan several times a day so water would not overflow on the floor. I was also charged with placing a sign in the front window of the house whenever we needed more ice. This sign had the numerals twenty-five printed in large letters on one side and fifty on the reverse side to signal the pounds of ice to be delivered. I placed this in the front window early in the morning so the iceman would deliver a new chunk that day. At the age of seventy-nine I still refer to a refrigerator as an "icebox" after fifty-five years of enjoying modern "fridges."

Daily my stepmother gave me a list of groceries or meats she needed from the store. I walked across the street, handed the list to the grocer and he would walk around the store collecting the items, place them in a bag and give me change. This was repeated next door at the meat market where no meat was cut until customers came in and ordered a specific amount of pork chops, cold meat or a two-pound roast. No self-service in those days!

When I reached ten or eleven, and had a steadier hand, another job was to take in the milk from the milkman. Milk was delivered to the house, not purchased from the grocery store. Every bottle of milk, whole milk in those days, came in glass bottles with about three inches of cream at the top. I carefully removed the paper cap from the top of the bottle and poured the cream into a separate container to be used in coffee or for whipping cream. It's a bit of a miracle I have lived to seventy-nine when I consider all the rich whole milk, rich ice cream, bacon, eggs and food fried in lard that I consumed growing up.

I was given a wagon when I was about four years old, a scooter at about seven and a bike at about ten or eleven. That was my only bike, a Western Flyer, from a company long gone from the retail world. I disassembled it every two or three weeks, greased and cleaned it from front to back, and that one bike lasted me until I purchased a used car at the age of sixteen. The car was a 1930 Model A Ford Roadster, price thirty dollars. When I went in military service at the age of seventeen, I sold it for fifteen dollars!

Cars were easy to fix in those days. There was a lot of space in the engine compartment. I could repair almost anything on that Ford with only a background in bicycle maintenance. Gas was about eleven cents a gallon. It was not uncommon to pull into a station and ask the attendant to put in a dime's worth of gas.

The average family had just one automobile. Streetcars provided the public transportation. We lived on a streetcar line that was handy for service but very noisy. The streetcars had steel wheels that ran on steel tracks in the middle of the street. The middle of the street in front of our house was about forty feet from our living room and the bedroom where I slept. When a car rumbled by, which was about every fifteen minutes during the day, more often at rush hours, and every hour-on-the-hour from midnight to six a.m., it was impossible to carry on a conversation or listen to the radio. We were used to this, however, and never complained that some government agency should buy our house, insulate it better or move the streetcar line. We felt fortunate to have the transportation.

Minneapolis had a triple-A minor league baseball team in the thirties and stars like Ted Williams, the "Splendid Splinter" (a reference to how thin he was), played with the "Millers," as they were called, on their way to the major leagues. I could get into the games for two or three Wheaties box tops one day each week or by joining the Knothole Club for a dime or fifteen cents on other designated days. The club played in a park that was user-friendly (the spectators were close to the field) but not symmetrical. The right field fence was only 279 feet down the foul line and we usually had a right fielder that was a "good bat, no field" type and played with his back resting against the right field wall. Many of our right fielders were slightly overweight and had numerous "hard nights," brought on by overindulgence in various beverages, so some needed the support. Triple-A baseball in those days was a mixture of promising rookies on the way up and aging veterans on the way down. An eclectic group! But everybody loved their local team and they didn't need a grandiose stadium to enjoy it in. Win or lose, the hometown team were heroes or bums but the fans were always behind them.

We revered all of our sports figures. The sixteen major league baseball teams in the country were the whole show in major league sports. Professional football, basketball and hockey hadn't spread to many cities at that time. Consequently the local college teams were our major interest. The University of Minnesota Golden Gophers football team received most of our adulation and everyone, on Saturday afternoons in the fall, had their ears glued to the radio to hear about the "Gophers." Major sports figures in the depression years stayed out of jail and out of trouble and college athletes in particular were idolized.

My main recreation in the evening was listening to the radio. It was a large Philco, popular at that time, a console on legs. The cabinet was wood. There were not many controls on those radios, only a simple station selection dial and a volume control knob. Below that was a speaker. This Philco, however, was considered state-of-the-art and we were proud of it. We had only one so I was allowed to hear some Buck Rogers, Little Orphan Annie, Renfrew of the Mounted or Jack Armstrong the All-American Boy programs at the dinner hour and then the adults took over for the evening. Some evenings, from eight o'clock to sign-off time, there would be only band music, a different band playing each half-hour. It would be a mixture of popular local bands with more famous East Coast or Chicago bands later in the evening. It was quite a contrast from today's sitcoms that fill our evening hours.

At about the age of thirteen I finally saved enough to buy my own radio for $9.95 after looking at it through the window of a downtown store for several months. I believe the outside was Bakelite, a type of plastic commonly used for small size radio cabinets in those days, and more attractive than the dull gray, formless-looking cabinets of today that remind one of cheap plastics. It was loaded with vacuum tubes and sounded better than most present-day radios. I always liked the big band sound that flourished at that time. At night I would listen to bands from ballrooms located on the east coast, primarily New York and New Jersey. The announcer would start the program with, "The music of Glen Miller is coming to you tonight from Frank Dailey's Meadowbrook on Route 23 at the Newark-Pompton Turnpike in Cedar Grove, New Jersey," or "This is the music of Artie Shaw direct from the Glen Island Casino in New Rochelle, New York." I would dream about the time when I could travel to those places and hear it all in person including the bands of Tommy and Jimmy Dorsey, Woody Herman and Count Basie to name just a few. Late at night, if I was really lucky, I might pick up a broadcast of Billie Holiday from somewhere in Manhattan and wonder how anyone could sing so poignantly.

When not in school, my stepmother and I always listened to "Ma Perkins" on the radio in the afternoon and marveled at how, in fifteen minutes, she solved all the problems in her family and her lumberyard business while following the principles of hard work, thriftiness, honesty and trust in God. We also learned, from her advertiser, about the magic of the very popular Oxydol soap. The phrase "Oxydol" became almost a generic for wash-day soap. Incidentally, that's where the name "soaps" came from that are today's "Guiding Light" or "One Life to Live." In the 1930s these fifteen minute daytime programs were called "serials" and we usually listened to one or two more, most notably "Fiber McGee and Molly," and laughed out loud at Fibber's inept antics at 79 Wistfull Vista Ave. and Molly's attempts to straighten him out. I believe Pepper Young's Family, Vic and Sade and Myrt and Marge soaps joined this lineup in later years.

These were precious times for a boy growing up. Problems abounded for the adults around me but the solutions were usually hard work, honesty and faith in one's religion.

Grade school, junior high and high school were memorable for dedicated teachers doing their best to excite unexcitable students along with a few promising scholars. My favorite teacher was a young woman who had a passion for Shakespeare and helped me enjoy a course that few high school students admitted enjoying at that time. There were no discipline problems in the schools. There were poor students, even students who failed courses and dropped from school, but no students with bad behavior typical of students that plague our schools today. Good order was normal, taken for granted. Bad behavior, in those years, was an abnormality.

Speed skating was a popular sport in the 1930s. It flourished in towns like Minneapolis, Milwaukee and smaller communities in the Midwest. A few blocks from our house was a park named Powderhorn Park with a lake in the middle of it and an island in the center of the lake. When the ice froze, this was a natural course for speed skating meets, and amateurs and professionals from all over the country gathered there for races on Sunday afternoons. Attendance frequently soared to ten thousand people on pleasant winter days and the results of the races were headline news in the Monday sports pages. It is a graceful sport for both men and women and exciting to watch the skaters come around the curves, effortlessly placing one leg over the other. Now the only speed skating that draws crowds is every four years at the Winter Olympics.

And then there were the movie theatres, lots and lots of movie theatres. Every neighborhood had a theatre just like every neighborhood had a church. There was only one screen but the picture changed every two or three days. A new one began on Monday and Tuesday, changed for Wednesday and Thursday and then again for Friday, Saturday and Sunday. The blockbusters, the really big attractions with the most popular actors and actresses, were reserved for the weekend. Tuesday was bank-night. There was a drawing, usually for fifteen or twenty-five dollars, and usually a full house in attendance. That was a lot of money in the thirties. The neighborhood theatres and a handful of downtown theatres played first-run, "A" movies. Several downtown theatres, plus all the neighborhood theatres, played "B" movies for Saturday afternoon matinees. These were mostly "horse operas," as they were called, Westerns with little dialogue but a lot of scenes with men on horses chasing each other. Double-features (two shows) were common and youngsters gained admittance for five cents. When I think about it now, how we sat through three to four hours of that "entertainment" defies memory.

The thirties were the heyday of motion pictures and Hollywood. Life was tough for most citizens and watching beautiful, elegantly dressed legends on a screen for two hours, for fifteen or twenty cents, was an escape few people could resist. The plots were usually love stories where the audience could fantasize themselves in the place of the hero or heroine. Later in the decade Hollywood reproduced spectacular Broadway shows, the dancing duos of Rogers and Astaire, Bing Crosby musicals and the Marx Brothers, Ritz Brothers and Andy Hardy comedies to name just a few. It was a glorious period in the history of Hollywood and the fascination for the average moviegoer far surpassed the lure of violence and sex on today's screen. Moviegoers in the thirties were looking for love and laughter. In the present decade they're waiting to be shocked and frightened.

The Great Depression years were a simple time in the best sense of that word. I remember when I fell off a garage in our backyard at the age of five- or six-years-old and cut a gash in my cheek. My stepmother picked me up and carried me across the street to a hospital where I was quickly stitched up and soon back home. I'm not claiming everyone lived across from a hospital but almost everyone had access to one in less than ten minutes. There were a dozen hospitals in Minneapolis in those years for a population a fraction of today's. Now there are four or five hospitals scattered miles apart, requiring long ambulance rides after calling 911.

Children grew slowly. We were respectful of our parents, in fact, of all adults. We listened to them and obeyed them. Of course there were problem children, difficult children, but not like the average child today who tells their parents what they will do, instead of the parent telling them. It was inconceivable that a young child would suggest to their parents how they should be dressed. I have a picture of myself at the age of four dressed in a short-pant, jump-suit style outfit with long stockings, belt-buckle shoes and bobbed hair, sitting on a piano bench with my arms holding one leg on the bench, the other leg on the floor. It's not my favorite picture but it sits today in a prominent place in my home because other members of the family apparently consider it so unusual for children of that age in contrast to today's demeanor.

One of my most vivid memories from early childhood were two trips from Minneapolis to North Dakota to attend the funerals of my paternal grandfather and grandmother. They were living on a farm in central North Dakota where good cropland ceases and ranch land begins. My father was trying to raise wheat and barley on that marginal land.

My grandfather died in 1930 at the age of eighty, my grandmother in 1935 at the age of eight-six. I have no memories of my grandfather. I only remember my grandmother, on the occasion of my grandfather's funeral, as a small, erect, Spartan-looking woman sitting in a chair in the kitchen saying very little while my father prepared meals for all of us.

I saw my father infrequently in these years, a circumstance I regret very much. Part of the reason was five hundred miles on single-lane roads. The other part was a depression that limited time and money for trips. We traveled by train, three different ones, to reach the town nearest the farm. That was the heyday of train travel, when you could reach any town in the country, if you were willing to change trains often, and sleep sitting up.

The farm was a bleak picture. The house, a small, square first floor with a couple of second floor rooms under a gable roof, was surrounded by a dilapidated barn and several small, nondescript chicken, hog and toolshed houses and the ubiquitous outhouse. The only trees in sight were in a small grove between the gravel road and the farm buildings. It was a desolate picture. If one had owned a telescope, I'm certain you could have seen as far as the curvature of the earth allowed.

It didn't cross my mind then, but it has dozens of times later, how much my father gave up when he allowed my aunt to take me, after my birth mother died, so he could care for his aged parents. Was I lucky or unlucky to escape that austere environment for life in a bustling city? Probably lucky, but why does everything that happens to us often come at a high price to those around us? Years later, long after my father died, I was on a trip to North Dakota (which I will discuss later in this book) and stopped at the farm my father had sold some years earlier when he retired. I spent an afternoon with the people who had bought it. They were still in contact with the hired man that worked for my father during most of the World War II years when my father was in physical decline after fifty years of hard manual labor. I talked to this "hired man" on the telephone, now in his nineties, but with a clear memory, and he said to me, "August, you have no idea how proud your father was of you during the War. Whenever someone would visit us on the farm, he would pick up a snapshot of you in uniform that your stepmother had sent to him and say, with obvious pride in his voice and manner, 'I have a son in service, you know. Here's his picture.' He really was proud of you."

Tears came to my eyes when I heard this because it brought home to me the loneliness and isolation my late father must have endured all those years, after he had given me to my aunt, in that desolate environment of rural farm life on the prairies.

I had a paternal aunt and uncle in Minneapolis who owned a grocery store several miles from our house whom we visited frequently on Sunday afternoons. Grocery stores weren't open on Sunday but my aunt and uncle lived in the back of their store so I had easy access to run around the premises if I wished. I never did. Instead I sat quietly, while my folks visited, knowing that sometime during the visit my aunt would take me by the hand, lead me out into the store and to the cookie display. There she would say, "What cookie would you like? You can have two or three if you wish."

Cookies in those days weren't wrapped in small cellophane packages or small boxes. They were delivered by a cookie wholesaler in cardboard boxes about a foot square and a foot deep and packed in rows of several layers. Each cardboard container would hold hundreds of cookies and each grocer had a large metal cookie rack that held probably nine or twelve boxes. Each rack opening had individual glass lids on a hinge that opened up for access to the treats. A customer told the grocer they wanted three or six or ten or a dozen, or whatever quantity, and the grocer picked that amount and placed them in a small sack. The number of flavors in the rack (the kind of cookies) was restricted to the rack's capacity for large twelve-inch by twelve-inch cartons – not much of a choice by today's selection possibilities.

After my selection my aunt would steer me back to her living quarters where I sat quietly munching the cookies and listening to the adults talk until it was time for us to leave.

Lest you think there was no excitement in our lives, however, I remember one hazardous practice in my childhood, even at the early age of eight years and up, and that was playing with fireworks on the Fourth of July. Fireworks were sold legally in Minnesota in the 1930s and were widely available to children of my age. I blew up tin cans and other containers with small firecrackers and large "cherry bombs," as they were called. We competed for several days during that time period to see who could blow a can the highest or crack it open the quickest. It was a stupid practice and one that cost thousands of children and young people their fingers, and even their eyes, until a crusade against fireworks by a local newscaster resulted in passage of a law banning them.

But, for me, the overall contrast of my childhood with today's children is stark. I grew up, and was content, to do "quiet" things. I had a stamp collection and bought what might be called "grab bags" of stamps from magazine advertisements for a quarter or fifty cents. I would sort through these bundles, most of the stamps of no value, looking for a few I didn't already own, or from a foreign country, and then painstakingly mount them in my stamp book. It was fun and exciting to discover stamps from countries I didn't know existed, find the countries on my small "globe" of the world and daydream about what kind of people lived there and wonder if I would ever be able to travel to those parts of the world.

I also read voraciously, everything I could get my hands on. My family were not great readers, except for the daily newspapers, but they knew I loved to read and bought me books on every occasion, birthdays, holidays and, frequently, just because they found one they thought I might enjoy. These were the years of serial books for young people. An author would begin to write a book about a young boy or girl and then add a book to the series for every few years of that person's life. I loved baseball, more than any other sport, and remember a series of books called *Baseball Joe*. There was *Baseball Joe on the School Nine*, *Baseball Joe on the Silver Stars*, *Baseball Joe in the Minors* and on and one until he made the major leagues as I remember.

I even read most of Edgar Allan Poe's books, despite their adult comprehension level, as my folks owned a complete set. His *"The Murders in the Rue Morgue,"* a tale of multiple, gruesome murders in an old house of unusual construction in Paris, was especially exciting and much too adult for a ten-or-eleven-year-old, but pale in comparison to the steady stream of violence and horror movies today's young people have available, Interestingly, Edgar Allan Poe, who was born in 1809 and died at the young age of forty after a life marred by poverty, illness, drinking and immorality, is considered by some to be the father of the detective genre, which we now call mysteries. Maybe I was more perceptive at that young age than I realized.

My folks would be aghast, however, after they gave me several books, and I announced I had read them all two or three days later. Young people today would probably consider *"Baseball Joe"* too elementary for their tastes but this difference defines the two periods. In the 1930s children were allowed to "age" naturally with a minimum of profanity, little violence and no sexual exploits in front of them in private life or in school.

The rubbish and tripe with which children are bombarded today bodes ill for our next generation.

I believe a final snapshot of my world in 1932 in Minnesota, when I was eight years old, would illuminate those years for the reader. At the grocery store a pound-and-one-half loaf of white bread was five cents. That's right! Five cents! A one pound loaf was four cents. We didn't have whole wheat or any dark bread in 1932 but "graham" bread came soon, a darkish-colored bread that looked a lot like white bread. Some stores had raisin bread but that was seven cents a loaf.

Butter was nineteen cents a pound, beans nine cents a can, soap five cents a bar, corn flakes ten cents a box, eggs thirteen cents a dozen and a ten pound bag of sugar forty-one cents. New automobile tires were about four dollars, a good quality men's suit was eight dollars and "extra thick, extra rich, extra smooth chocolate malted milk (with wafers)" was five cents at my favorite drug store soda fountain. And every drug store had a soda fountain. Where else could Hollywood find its new starlets?

Besides the Chryslers, Chevrolets and Fords, popular cars were Auburn, Essex, Graham, Huppmobile, Nash, Oakland, Whippet (we had one of those), Paige and Durant. Used car ads usually were headed with a teaser: "$1.99 buys a Ford Tudor Sedan" and they had one on the lot for that price. A 1932 advertisement listed a two-year-old 1930 Dodge Sedan for $499 and a three-year-old 1929 Pontiac Deluxe Coupe for $299. New cars were only several hundred dollars more but few were buying. Iceboxes (they were beginning to call them refrigerators) sold for $16.95 for a fifty-pound size, $19.95 for seventy-five-pound and $23.95 for one-hundred-pound. The difference was the size or weight of the chunk of ice that would fit in the ice compartment.

Headlines in the daily papers centered on whether the Eighteenth Amendment to the Constitution of the United States, which instituted prohibition of intoxicating liquors, should be repealed (it was in 1933 by the Twenty-first Amendment). Other hot topics were how to pay for public works, was the gold standard responsible for the depression, and a surprising amount of news about Adolf Hitler who became chancellor of Germany the following year. The country tracked Hitler fairly well in that decade. They just turned their backs on doing anything about it until he had conquered almost all of Europe and was eyeing the rest of the world.

Other headlines were the upcoming political conventions. Herbert Hoover was the President of the United States but soon to be replaced by Franklin Roosevelt in the November, 1932 elections and inaugurated in January of 1933. Yo-Yo tournaments were the rage, (that flat, round piece of wood tied to a string and propelled up and down – "like a Yo-Yo"). That's where the expression originates. Dance marathons lasted for hours and even days. The winner was the last couple standing and presumably still moving. In the movies were Tallulah Bankhead, Constance Bennett, Greto Garbo, Paul Muni, James Cagney, Douglas Fairbanks, Jr. and Tom Mix (and his faithful horse Tony). If you're under fifty today, you may be surprised at the longevity of some of the movie stars of that period. Today stars shine for a few years and are gone. In those days many stars came on as children and survived to old age.

But the really big story in 1932 was the grasshopper plague. Agriculture was characterized by one disaster after another, oftentimes a new one each year, i.e., drought, sand storms, surpluses, low prices, grasshoppers, other bugs, etc. The June 14, 1932 edition of the *Minneapolis Tribune* newspaper framed the problem succinctly. Below a picture of a farmer's field with nothing in it, except furrows of dirt, a caption read, "This barley field on the farm of [name omitted] in the fertile grain country to the southwest of Fargo, N.D., waved a bright promise of opulence and plenty before the 'hopper horde' began its destructive work. The verdant sprouts were eaten swiftly away, leaving barren rows of cultivated earth to mark the trail of the pest. The grasshopper is no respecter of any particular growing grain, however, for wheat, rye, oats and all manner of growing crops suffer equally."

A sidebar outlined the grasshopper's alarming, prodigious propagation capabilities. It read,

"One female grasshopper in 1929. Fifty-four million grasshoppers in 1932. That is the estimated propagation of one northwest grasshopper in the period of four years, according to Professor [name omitted] of the entomology division, University of Minnesota. [He said] 'In the grasshopper outbreak there are always half a dozen species which predominate. We will take the two-lined grasshopper, the big fellow who is doing the most damage in the northwest. Due to suitable weather conditions we can safely estimate that the female had 600 eggs in 1929. In 1930 the eggs would hatch. Half would be female. With 300 females hatching 600 eggs apiece, in the spring of 1931 there would be 180,000 grasshoppers. Half of the 180,000 would be female. The 90,000 female grasshoppers would hatch 600 eggs apiece. And in 1932 there would be 54,000,000 grasshoppers, ready to start their attack on the farmer's fields' All from one grasshopper. But many grasshoppers are in the business of propagation, and the fight is not on 54,000,000 but endless billions!"

That may be more than you wish to know about grasshoppers but this is one example where statistics don't lie and vividly illustrate the enormity of the problem for farmers in those years.

The states appropriated money to fight them, and there were calls to Congress to assist with the financial burden. The answer to the problem, finally, was a change in the natural cycle of life. Be it animal, human or the weather, apparently everything on this globe moves in cycles.

In 1933 the National Industrial Recovery Act (NRA), a law enacted by Congress, was one of the measures to assist the nation's economic woes during this Great Depression. The act authorized drafting a set of codes for each of more than five-hundred industries, suspending relevant antitrust regulations, setting codes of industrial conduct and containing a maximum-hour workday and minimum wage provisions. The NRA reflected divergent goals and suffered from widespread criticism, however. The codes did little to help recovery and in 1935 the U.S. Supreme Court nullified them as an unconstitutional delegation of legislative power. The NRA was abandoned.

What lessons can we learn today from those troubled times? One lesson is there are cycles to all conditions in this world (from grasshoppers to the stock market). When it looks the darkest, persistence, honesty, hard work and optimism may be all we have so why not fall back on those qualities? They were abundant in the 1930s. They are disappearing today. We need to bring them back.

Symptomatic of this deterioration in self-reliance is the current trend to supply school bus transportation for all students. A Minnesota Congressman who is pushing a federal program called "safe routes" (to encourage more school walking and biking programs), reported recently that, "In the past forty years the number of kids walking to school has fallen from sixty percent to ten percent, and the number riding bikes has dropped from twenty-five percent to two percent."

Those are alarming statistics by anyone's calculation. The Congressman went on to say, "Twenty-five percent of children fifteen and under are clinically obese. Seventy-five percent of trips children fifteen and under take are by vehicle …They're mobility-challenged. We need to change that."

One caveat to more walking, of course: Watch out for the pedophiles who have probably increased by alarming percentages in the past forty years!

Are there lessons to be learned from the Great Depression days? Yes, there are. We need to instill patience, obedience and an even temperament in our children. Responsibility for child-rearing is not a "village." It's a mother and father who tell it not to be afraid, love it, care for it, say "no" when necessary and give it an example to follow. And don't ask a four-year-old where it wants to go or what it wants to eat. Tell it gently and firmly and expect obedience!

♦ Chapter Two: **TEEN YEARS**

There will be some chronological overlap in all these chapters. The readers are asked for patience to this anomaly. Life is not easily bracketed. One period tends to flow into another but the teen years presented some distinctive opportunities and challenges for contrast with the present.

There was little money in my teens. From age twelve to seventeen (1936 to 1941) I had maybe a dollar or two to spend each week. Part time jobs paying fifteen or twenty cents per hour were scarce. Adults at full time, mid-level jobs earned only eighty dollars a month. The discrepancy was more than inflation. It was fewer jobs for smaller rewards.

In contrast, in 2001, the average American teen spent over one hundred dollars a week. They all have credit cards (or will have as soon as they enter college) and are usually in debt. One in four owns a cell phone and in a few years that ratio is forecasted to rise to three of four. They come to breakfast at high school and want cappuccino. Regular coffee isn't strong enough! Maybe that attitude, that expectation they should have everything as a teenager, contributes to why an alarming percentage admit they have thought about killing themselves and why the suicide rate is so high. Last year in the Midwest a teen was arrested for trying to poison his father because he wanted "a new computer room" his father was unwilling to provide.

There was only one fast food hamburger chain in the 1930s with perhaps two or three outlets in several major cities. There were one-owner "chicken shacks" serving fried chicken, and general menu restaurants, but it was rare for families to eat meals away from home. Money was tight for home-cooked meals leaving nothing for restaurants.

A friend of mine, my age, remembers the poverty of those years that affected all of us. Vivid in his recollection is the time he went to the grocery store for a neighbor who was unable to go herself. When he returned, she paid him a nickel for the errand. He immediately went back to the store and bought a loaf of bread for his family who had no bread at that time. He remembers how proud he was when he was able to hand that loaf of bread to his mother.

This friend's wife remembers her father working in a local flour mill that turned out a cereal product popular in those days. It was shipped in a large, cotton flour-style sack highly prized by the workers for all the ways in which slightly irregular sacks could be recycled. Her mother made dishtowels, wash cloths, pillow cases, even underwear from those flour sacks. The employees were also allowed to take home as much of the cereal product as they wished each day and this wife remembers when that was all they had to eat at home. There would be cereal for breakfast (with a bit of milk), fried cereal for dinner (the name of the mid-day meal those years), probably with some lard or fat spread on it, and again for supper (the name for the evening meal), doctored up in some manner to provide a hint of difference.

In the city, running water and inside bathrooms were common in the house but in the country they were rare. People in the country relied on a large garden to supply much of their food. In the city the lots were usually so small there was little room for gardens.

It was not uncommon for teens to work for no payment. In 1934 and 1935 my stepmother had serious operations in the summer requiring long convalescences and I was sent to spend the summer with an aunt and uncle in Des Moines, Iowa. The aunt and uncle had two sons who owned and operated a grocery store and I helped them in the store. My payment was all the cold pop I could drink. That was it.

Des Moines was also the site of one of my most memorable recollections of the severity of the Great Depression. Twice each week one of my cousins running the store loaded up all the stale, spoiled, frequently rotten produce they could not sell and transported it to the town dump. The dump bordered the Des Moines River not far from downtown. Many black families lived in and around this dump. As my cousin and I approached the dump small children as young as four and five years would recognize our truck and run to get first pickings at the spoiled produce. They were so hungry they fought off the constantly circling dump birds for the better pieces. This scene, repeated numerous times, will always live in my memory. Today's welfare support system, compared to those dump scenes, is one contrast highly in favor of our present methods for feeding children in need.

But those were good summers, tranquil summers, I will never forget and symbolic of that period when we didn't have many worldly possessions but a lot of peace and love and appreciation of small favors. One of my aunt's sons who operated the grocery store delivered grocery orders twice a day in a panel truck to people who ordered by phone. Home delivery is being touted as innovative today. In those years it was routine. I usually accompanied him on the route and quickly learned the streets and avenues all over Des Moines. We would stop for breakfast in the morning and usually some refreshment in the afternoon. It was a great opportunity for conversation with my cousin, now long deceased, of course, and I remember him fondly today. One's memories, especially the good ones, are made of small things, I believe, not only the cataclysmic events.

Even the grocery store was a symbol of those simpler times. One brand of food dominated among all the canned goods, one bakery delivered all the bread. Fresh meat, baked goods and pharmaceuticals were carried in other stores, not in grocery stores. Most of the customers were on charge accounts. When a customer called for a delivery, a charge slip was handwritten listing each item and its price and totaled at the bottom using a cumbersome adding machine or frequently in the grocer's head. One learned to add columns of numbers quickly in those days.

These slips were all housed in large, black metal trays with a compartment for each account and a spring on the top of each compartment that snapped down to hold all the slips in place. At the end of the month the slips were totaled and the grocer either waited for the customer to come into the store and pay something on his or her account or give a payment to my cousin when he delivered an order. Statements were rarely mailed to a customer. Postage was two or three cents, a significant sum in those days, and statements were considered somewhat of an affront to the customer. After all, it was understood: "I know I owe you money. If I had any, I'd pay you so don't remind me." I realize that attitude seems unrealistic today but that's what the 1930s were like. We were all poor, in resources at least, but because the problem was universal, we didn't realize we were so poor. We maintained our pride. That pride was instrumental in getting us through that difficult period.

I traveled from Minneapolis to Des Moines on trains known affectionately as "streamliners." These were passenger trains that ran between major cities with few stops in-between. Their heyday was from about 1934 to the beginning of World War II. These streamliners became very popular because regular passenger train service, available to every small town on the map, required multiple train changes and several days to reach a destination.

When this fast service between major cities began, it required only some improved engines and lightweight passenger cars. The roadbed (the tracks) were already in place – unlike today where we have allowed much of our roadbed to disintegrate to the point where trains must travel over it slowly to avoid derailments. Most of the passenger cars were built of aluminum with a sleek, gleaming appearance, thus the name "streamliners" came into use. This premium service continued until the War when manufacturers of these trains were converted to war production of freight cars, troop sleepers, hospital cars or tanks, planes or other weapons needed in the war effort. For a stroll down memory lane, an industrial advertisement from those years included the following railroads in its lineup of customers:

The Atchison, Topeka & Santa Fe Railway Co.
Bangor & Aroostook Railroad Co.
Boston & Maine Railroad
Chicago & North Western Railway Co.
The Chicago, Rock Island & Pacific Railway Co.

Great Northern Railway Co.
Illinois Central Railroad Co.
The Kansas City Southern Railway Co.
Lehigh Valley Railroad Co.
The New York Central Railroad Co.
Norfolk & Western Railway Co.
The Pennsylvania Railroad Co.
St. Louis Southwestern Railway Co.
Seaboard Railway
Southern Pacific Railroad Co.
Southern Railway System
Union Pacific Railroad Co.

How many of these names exist today? Very few. Their decline is consistent with what's happened to our train service in the intervening years.

There were never any guns or dangerous knives in my junior or senior high schools. The possibility was unthinkable. Some boys carried Boy Scout knives but they were never used for any purpose inconsistent with Boy Scout programs. I felt safe, secure and at ease in school at all times. No hats were worn or allowed in the classroom and discipline was the responsibility of the individual teacher. Most teachers handled this adequately. On rare exceptions a teacher allowed some mild prankishness when his or her back was turned but the misbehavior never went beyond that level. Discipline began with the gym teacher. Usually a man for the boys and a woman for the girls, they led the students through calisthenics and games without tolerating any dissent or protestations. If the student failed to participate with some enthusiasm, he or she may have been "helped" to sit down on a chair in full view of the class for the remainder of the period. The next step up was the principal and that was the ultimate threat. Having to see him or her was to be avoided at all costs. There were no security personnel or school police liaison.

The stark contrast between today's schoolroom atmosphere of disrespect and the classes of my era is a primary difference in the two periods. It is also a difference that should serve warning for the dangerous path we are following at the present time.

Youth centers were widely available to teens in Minneapolis. They had pool and ping-pong tables, various other games, jukeboxes for dancing and a soft drink and snack bar. No drugs or liquor were allowed and rarely a consideration or threat by the teens who used the centers. They were funded by various private and charitable organizations and are a concept highly in need in today's environment.

The teen music of choice was the big band sound of Glen Miller, Artie Shaw, Duke Ellington, Harry James and Louis Armstrong to name just a few. The big bands rarely traveled as far off the beaten track as Minnesota but we listened nightly to their broadcasts emanating from the famous hotels and ballrooms across the country and fantasized about one day hearing our musical idols in person.

The vocalists in these bands sang songs where the lyrics were clear and understandable and usually dealt with love lost or retained. This was "sweet" music, sometimes fast or jazzy, but more often slow and sentimental. Few young people possessed the money to buy records, old plastic 78s, but we could go to a small hamburger shop or restaurant and play our favorite tunes all evening for five cents a play.

Thus the 1930s were a reassuring time for teens. The music was comforting, the streets and schools safe, dating easy and unhurried, families intact and the radio (there was no television) mostly clean soap operas and comedies.

Much of today's teen music, however one attempts to justify it, is brutal, hostile, demeaning and unintelligible. The difference in the music of these two periods is a significant reason the 1930s is "a forgotten world" to which we sorely need a return.

Nothing is perfect, however, and there is one huge advantage to today's world: that is the opportunity for women to participate in athletics during their teen years and beyond. Women were not given an opportunity to participate in high school varsity sports and, on their own time, only in tennis and golf. It's fortunate we have corrected that injustice.

Information, as a resource, was available from books in libraries and there were a lot of libraries, one in almost every neighborhood. This promoted reading books, which is a lost art to too many teens today, but it doesn't compare with the data available on today's Internet. Whether that is good or bad depends on how much time teens spend using the Internet wisely versus time spent on games and sex.

Overall, I believe teens in the 1930s grew up more respectful, more balanced, less problem-plagued than teens now. They may not have had their heads crammed with all of today's sights and sounds but too much of these are irrelevant and probably damaging to their future.

One example from my young years is illustrative of this difference. As a ten-year-old I couldn't afford a real, genuine radio so I purchased a do-it-yourself kit for a crystal radio from a mail order catalog for a price so low I can't remember what it was. I assembled the radio and listened to it with headphones by operating an arm with a wire pointer on it, which I believe was called a cat's whisker, over a small receptacle holding some type of crystal material. All it would receive were one or two local stations. The chance of returning to the same station on successive evenings was unlikely but, regardless of the source, it was real live music. I was overjoyed to have it. The reaction of today's ten-year-old at such a possession is unfortunately predictable.

There were innumerable other ways our life was different. We had two mail deliveries Monday through Friday, one in the morning, one in the afternoon, and a morning delivery on Saturday. The newspapers offered a diversity of opinion not available now in most metropolitan areas. For teens just beginning to pay attention to local, national and world events, this was critical.

A memory that will always be with me is watching homeless men regularly come to our back door asking for something to eat. Unemployment at the height of the depression in the early- and mid-thirties was about forty percent. Thousands of these men were continually on the move, riding boxcars on the rail lines, searching for work. There was a railroad line running east and west through South Minneapolis two blocks from our house. If the railroad slowed, these men would jump off and fan out over the neighborhood knocking on doors for something to eat. My mother never turned them away. She always managed to find a slice of mush left over from our breakfast or a slice of bread with jelly or lard on it for a sandwich. These men would thank her for this handout and a drink of water from the outside faucet and sit quietly in our yard eating their food while I shot baskets, played catch or other games nearby. Not once was I ever bothered or threatened by these men.

My family never owned their own home. We rented, usually in a duplex or fourplex. But these were the years of extreme heat in the summer and extreme cold in the winter that set numerous weather records. That's one reason we had the Great Depression, at least on the farms. Weather extremes were routine. I remember one fourplex where we occupied one of the upper flats. There must not have been any insulation in the ceiling because the temperature in our house was so high we had to spend most of the summer, three adults and me, living in the basement sleeping on cots. The high temperature for the day, and for days at a time, would be above one-hundred degrees and higher inside the flat where there was little air movement and no air conditioning, of course. My mother would run up to the flat several times a day to get some food but other than that it was really untenable up there. As a young boy I did not suffer unduly but the adults had a difficult time. The occupants of the other upper flat in the fourplex lived with us in the basement, not a good arrangement for all involved.

In the winter it was in excess of twenty below zero for days on end. There wasn't anti-freeze for automobiles as there is today. The only protection was to mix alcohol with water for the radiator of the car. Alcohol has a low boiling point and the radiator would overheat easily on warmer days or long trips. Heaters inside the car were unreliable and balky and the best protection against the cold was to bring blankets and wrap them around your waist and legs on very cold days. In the city people relied on streetcars for transportation much of the winter. They never failed as they ran on electricity. On the farm, no farmer lived without a horse and buggy. If the old car wouldn't start, the horse would always go.

Young people today probably believe those days were horrible. They were not that bad. The physical hardships required cooperation between all of us to overcome them. That unified us in a manner difficult to explain. Hardships promote togetherness, I guess.

I will also never forget a scene from five years ago when I stood at the grave of an aunt I never knew who died in 1898 at the age of thirteen, almost three decades before I was born. I never knew this aunt existed until I found records of her birth and death while working on a restoration project at her parents' cemetery (my grandparents) in North Dakota in 1995. The grandparents were immigrants who settled initially in Iowa about 1878. My aunt was born to them in 1885 and died in 1898 from one of the many childhood diseases common in that period. In 1903 the family moved to North Dakota to homestead land offered in that state. That was just five years after my aunt's death.

I visited her grave in Iowa in 1998 and stood there transfixed as I tried to think back one hundred years and how the world had changed in that time and how this would have impacted her if she had lived. Undoubtedly her parents visited her gravesite from 1898, the year she died, to 1903, when they moved from Iowa to North Dakota, but I'm certain no one named Blegen ever stood at her grave from 1903 to 1998, a period of almost one hundred years. There were only dirt roads between North Dakota and Iowa in 1898, and for decades after that, and no one took that difficult journey unless it was absolutely essential. I felt honored, but also humble and so sad, to be the first relative to pay homage to her in all that time.

Today's teens drive that distance to see a friend or attend a concert and consider it a routine part of living. In this area, once again, my recollections are in stark contrast to the twenty-first century we live in now.

I did own an automobile in my senior year of high school, however, the 1930 Model A Ford Roadster mentioned previously. What a beauty! It was a rag top (convertible) with a rumble seat in the rear, painted gray with bright red trim. Seat belts were decades away from introduction and one rode around in that car, the top down, and maybe the rumble seat occupied, with a feeling of freedom and adventure I have never experienced in an automobile since that time. It didn't even have a radio. One could hum or sing one's own popular melodies as you drove along in the fresh air. That car today, in mint condition, would be almost priceless.

A friend of mine had a 1935 Plymouth, equally as popular as Fords or Chevrolets in those years, for which he paid $75 in 1938. That was considered a terrific car for a young man in those years and stirred envy from all teens not so fortunate.

But there is more to my teen years of the 1930s; for example, the subjects we had in school. In my sophomore year we covered English, geometry, Norwegian, United States history, auto mechanics and wood shop. My junior year focused on English, civics, United States history, Norwegian, bookkeeping and typing. The senior year I studied English, economics, sociology and bookkeeping.

Note the emphasis on English. It was the only required subject each year. The specific content was different each semester, for example, Shakespeare for half a year, but grammar was always highlighted. In addition to English, some of the above subjects were required at least one year but there were always two electives.

The teachers in high school concentrated on their subjects. There was no politicking in the classroom, no slanting the news or events of the day to fit a political ideology. The classrooms were only desks, chairs, books and blackboards. No machines, signs, notes or other debris were scattered about to distract students.

In recent years there have been several books by minority authors emphasizing how discriminatory life was in the 1930s in my area of the country. As I acknowledged previously I know some discrimination existed but I disagree it was rampant at the neighborhood level or in my high school. According to my yearbook there were five minority students in my graduating class. All five participated in at least one extra-curricular club or committee. One of the five participated in seven clubs or committees, another nine. I believe that represents adequate if not exemplary integration. That's several more, by the way, than the number in which I participated.

My high school was maintained squeaky clean. Students did not litter or mess it up and janitors worked diligently to keep it in repair. I remember visiting my old school in the 1970s just before it was demolished in favor of some higher conceived plan that escapes me at the moment. It was a multi-story building and so old the middle portion of each of the concrete steps was rounded down from years of wear. Inside, the entire school was spotless. In contrast, in a similar period, I visited my children's grade schools that had just been constructed and saw holes in the ceiling where children under the age of ten had apparently thrown items that punched these holes.

We also weren't being prepped for merely earning a living or getting a job in the 1930s. The objective was a well-rounded education. There were technical (we called them vocational) high schools in the city for students who wanted to emphasize those subjects. No sex education, no multicultural classes, no diversity training interfered with math, history and English.

A prominent theme running through all of these classes was a reverence for and appreciation of the country's historical figures, George Washington, Abraham Lincoln, Benjamin Franklin, Thomas Jefferson, Patrick Henry, Daniel Webster and the country's significant documents, The Declaration of Independence, the Constitution, Washington's speech at Valley Forge, and many more. The objective, I now understand, was to instill in us a feeling of pride and love for our country.

If there was anything lacking in this education, it was probably the absence of world history or world affairs. The opinion, to some degree, was this country was protected by two gigantic oceans and we had little to fear – or learn – from the world beyond. We were isolationists despite our experience in World War I and this carried through until the attack by Japan on Pearl Harbor on December 7, 1941. We were a sleeping giant and this attack woke us up. If we had studied, realized what was going on in other areas of the world prior to that, maybe we would have been better prepared for World War II. On the other hand communications of all types were crude compared to our technology today and that allowed us to largely ignore, or at least relegate to a secondary status, foreign affairs in our schools and in other communications such as newspapers, magazines and radio.

Organized athletics for young people were almost non-existent. If one made the high school teams, those teams were organized, and there were some youth baseball teams sponsored by the American Legion, but that was it. I lived a few blocks from a large park and I do remember playing on an intra-mural type park board hockey team for two winters when I was about twelve- or thirteen-years-old but they were probably organized because the high schools didn't have hockey at that time. Our only "equipment" was magazines strapped to our shins with rubber bands. Anyone dressed like our young hockey players today would have been considered a man (or woman) from Mars.

A friend, who was quite tall, remembers the basketball coach in junior high school asking him to try out for the team. He said he would like to but he had no shoes and couldn't afford to buy any. The coach dug up a used pair for him and my friend remembers taking them home, running all the way, to clean them up. They were black tennis shoes with white laces that he removed and scrubbed vigorously to get them spotlessly clean.

Local parks were geared to helping young people occupy their time playing sports, not hanging out on street corners looking for trouble. At the park near my house I could get the use of a basketball, baseball equipment, horseshoes and lots of other equipment, just by signing my name to a list maintained by the caretaker in the warming house (so-called because that's what it was for skaters in the cold winter months) and returning it when I was through playing. We were careful of all the items loaned to us because we valued their availability. If we damaged something, it might not be available again.

Young people organized their own games. In my neighborhood we had one or two empty lots in each block. We were fortunate if a block had two empty lots back to back that gave us more room. We tailored our games to whatever size space was available, however, and would play football and baseball for hours after dividing up into two teams whomever showed up. If too few came, we would have a kicking contest with the football or a baseball game where the batter was out if he hit it out of a narrowly defined area.

These were unorganized, irregular activities in comparison to the opportunities young people enjoy today.

It was difficult to get a job, part time or full time, in our teens. The best opportunity was delivering newspapers and magazines. We had three daily papers and dozens of magazines, some by mail but many by delivery boy. Sorry, girls didn't qualify. I'm not defending that, merely telling you how it was. But there were long waiting lines for the newspaper routes. I never achieved my own route but filled in for some of my friends when they were sick or on vacation.

Newspapers were delivered to hundreds of "paper shacks," as they were called, spread throughout the city. These shacks all constructed of corrugated sheet metal and about six feet square in size. They were unbearably hot in summer and unbearable cold in winter so one did not tarry longer than necessary to retrieve the papers. Large trucks from the newspaper company dumped bundles of papers in the shacks and the boys with the routes came there in the morning or afternoon to pick them up. It paid to arrive at the shack early so one could get enough papers to service his route. It was not uncommon for someone to take a few extra papers and sell them on the side, on the street corner. We were mostly honest in those days, but not perfect!

I did have a magazine route but traveled a wide area to deliver magazines with a price as low as five cents on the cover, for which I was paid two cents for delivering it. Part time jobs in a grocery store were the next possibility but during the depression days there were plenty of grown men with families, ready and eager to take those jobs before they were given to young people. That's one reason we became so skilled at baseball, football and basketball: We had nothing else to do!

Some feeling of despair was widespread. Jobs were scarce, money scarcer and the future dim. Many teens did not see the value of education and did not finish high school. Why study? There were no jobs. It was illogical to believe you could get a job without a high school diploma easier than with a diploma but that apparently never entered their thought processes.

The Federal Government in 1935 began the Works Progress Administration (WPA), a relief measure, providing money for a wide variety of programs, including highways and building construction, slum clearance, reforestation and rural rehabilitation. By mid-1936 the WPA rolls had provided work for over three million people and this program continued until 1943 when it was terminated. I also remember a program (because two of my high school friends dropped out of school to join it) named the Civilian Conservation Corp (or CCCs) paying thirty dollars a month plus board and room to young men desperate for work. As war clouds gathered in the late 1930s, however, and the armed forces needed recruits, men enlisted eagerly and that program was terminated. After the Japanese attack on Pearl Harbor on December 7, 1941, there was a flood of young boys clamoring to enlist. I was one of them. My high school class was graduating in January 1942, but after Pearl Harbor I wanted to enlist in the Navy and did so in late December, 1941. Thus my high school allowed me to leave about five weeks early with the promise of a diploma in January which they subsequently sent to my stepmother. The first four months in the Navy I earned twenty-one dollars per month. With room and board it wasn't bad pay in those days for a young man.

The Navy needed recruits so desperately that most of them were sent to training camp for only three weeks and then were assigned to duty aboard ships or other forward area locations. I was lucky to receive assignment to more specialized training after the first three weeks. The country felt it was under siege at that time and no extra weeks were allowed for training that could be postponed to a later date.

Despite the feeling of despair that prevailed in those years, however, teens were respectful of their elders, in fact, adults in general. My stepmother picked out most of my clothes for me until I joined the Navy at the age of seventeen. This would be unimaginable today. We ate whatever was set in front of us, at home, rarely in restaurants, and deferred to adults in our families on most every decision. Yes, there were some exceptions to this demeanor, some incorrigible teens, but I'm speaking of the average teen in those years.

My age group did have one bad habit, however. Before we could purchase – or afford – an automobile we perfected the practice of hopping streetcars, primarily at night, to get around the city. Streetcars were numerous, were all-electric, and on the back of the car there was a round container bolted to the outside. This carried the electrical current on a flexible pole up to the electric lines running above the car in the street. It was easy to grab hold of this container, or box, prop your feet against the car and ride it without being detected by the motorman in front. Streetcars were in the process of changing from a two-man motorman in front and conductor in the rear to just a one-man motorman-conductor in front, especially at night, so we weren't easily detected.

If this seems uncharacteristic to my portrayal of well-behaved youth of that era, remember that forty percent of the men in the country were unemployed during many of these years and traveled about the country hopping railroad cars, or boxcars as we called them, now known as a very dangerous practice. Was our streetcar-hopping, analogous to rail-car hopping, more dangerous than drugs or alcohol so prevalent today? I think not, but you're free to pick your poison. And this was a practice for a limited number of youths who had access to streetcar routes.

Young teens also had access to numerous pool halls that were often in back of beer joints. Laws for minors on those premises serving alcohol, were not as rigidly enforced but I'll wager youths of my age did far less illegal drinking than teens today who seem to find liquor available despite our current laws. Many obtain it today from affluent parents who are frequently not home.

That's where and how – in a pool hall in back of a beer joint where we were allowed to enter through the rear door – I learned to play snooker pool, a type almost a lost art now but a lot of fun. Snooker was played, as I remember, with one regular size white cue ball and fifteen smaller red balls but there are several variations of the game employing additional balls. We didn't drink beer, believe it or not, just played pool and there were fewer problems with minors drinking than we have today.

As in the last chapter I believe another "snapshot" will give you a better feel for life in my teens. Prices for groceries in 1937 were about the same as five years earlier. There were some new movie stars like Loretta Young, Deanna Durbin and Cary Grant, but most of the old stars were still appearing regularly. The price of cars had not increased significantly. A new Chevrolet was about $625 with "new Torpedo Rear-End Styling," said the ads. Moving up a bit, a new Nash was about $700. I will never forget the advertisements for new Nash cars that ran in pages like *Life* Magazine and similar publications. A typical ad would picture a sleek, stylish auto traversing a country road on the way to grandma's house. Below the picture were two slanted columns of copy in soothing expressions extolling the pleasure (not the virtue) of driving and owning this automobile. It was poetry in prose, a copywriter's best art. I don't know what advertising agency created those Nash ads but they should have been given the advertising equivalent of a Pulitzer Prize for their efforts.

It was a time when I began dreaming of driving and owning a car and I vowed to have a Nash some day. Believe it or not, I bought a used one some years after World War II and happily drove it for several more years.

Today most auto advertising, on television, of course, is mind numbing in its repetitive, sledgehammer tactics leaving nothing to the sensibilities except a strong desire to look the other way every time the commercial is run.

If you were traveling and needed to stay in a hotel, it was inexpensive. A middle-class hotel in midtown Manhattan in the mid-1930s was advertising weekly rates for single rooms with "running water, private lavatory" for $7 per WEEK, with private bath $10 per week. Daily rates were $1.50!

But some things never change. That old standby, Bayer Aspirin, was popular for many purposes and available in "a box of 12 tablets or bottle of 24 or 100 at any drugstore." Few branded products have had that exemplary staying power with the consumer.

Lastly, in our journey back to the late 1930s, if you had some money and owning your own home was your goal, how would you like this gem?: Five bedrooms, three baths, two-car garage, all brick and stone construction, in Metropolitan New York, and amenities like a large reception hall that opens to a 25-foot living room with a huge, log-burning fireplace, double casement doors open to a terrace and the garden, a dining room with its chairrail and paneled dado done in silver gray, waxed chestnut, kitchen with the latest appliances, bedroom and bath on first floor and four more bedrooms and two baths upstairs, a 17' by 22' porch, grounds exquisitely landscaped and membership in a nearby country club. Price: $11,990! If you can't pay cash, payments will be $89 a month. That was life then but not for everyone, of course.

Purveyors of misfortune were common, however, and editorials writers frequently warned homeowners with mortgages to be wary of speculators who had purchased mortgages from banks or other financial institutions for pennies on the dollar and would then "hover about the holders (the homeowners) ready to take unfair advantage of exaggerated distress."

But this was a defining period in United States history over and above my experience in it as a teen. The isolationist stance of the United States in the 1930s, then Pearl Harbor and the beginning of World War II, overshadowed all other events from 1929 to 1941. The reason is the Great Depression in this country was an economic problem, whereas World War II was a problem of survival of this country from its enemies. I hope the readers of this book will stay with me while I try to explain how the seriousness and sacrifice of the people at that time, including teenagers like myself, forever molded and shaped our lives.

How many people today would rate sacrifice for one's country the first priority in their lives? I shudder when I postulate the possibility of this country being threatened today by a force equal to Japan and Germany in 1941. Millions of people were asked to give up all – and I mean all – of their everyday needs like gas, tires, meat, coffee, clothes, vacations, and on and on, and work a seven-day week, many on the second and third shift (the night shift), while making these sacrifices. And agreeing to do this en masse without balking. I know some of us would do it but I fear a very large, very substantial percentage would say, "What the heck, we're not going to war if there's any possibility it can be avoided. Let's wait–and wait–and wait–and see what happens."

Well, we waited and waited in the 1930s and our enemies only became stronger. But we weren't alone. The major powers of Europe looked the other way while Adolf Hitler assumed power in Germany in 1933, regained control of the Saar in 1935, occupied Austria in 1938, and the Sudetenland (a region of Czechoslovakia) in 1938. It was this move by Hitler that prompted British Prime Minister Neville Chamberlain and French Prime Minister Edouardo Daladier, who signed an agreement with Hitler in 1938 allowing this takeover, called the Munich Pact, to announce on their return from the meeting with Hitler, the famous – or infamous – "peace in our time" guarantee. In 1939 Germany invaded the remainder of Czechoslovakia and then invaded Poland. So much for "peace in our time!" Finally, Britain and France declared war against Germany. In 1940 Germany invaded Norway, Denmark and France. In the latter half of that year the Nazis almost brought Britain to its knees with a savage air bombardment of London and surrounding areas. Ultimately it failed as Germany could not control the skies over England. While this was in progress, and Belgium and the Netherlands were overrun and occupied by Germany, rumors abounded of the persecution of the Jews in Germany and the horrible atrocities committed in the name of the (German) "superior race."

An ocean away, the United States decided they did not have justification to intervene militarily but they should have interceded more actively, with greater amounts of arms and supplies, for the countries fighting Germany. President Roosevelt, running for re-election in 1940, had promised the country he would never allow their sons to fight and die in a war on foreign soil. That was just what the country wanted to hear and made it easier to ignore a similar story emerging from the Pacific area.

Japan was engaged in its own expansion plans. In 1931 it invaded Manchuria and named it Manchukuo. In 1933 Japan resigned from the League of Nations (the counterpart to today's United Nations in some respects), and in 1937 invaded portions of China with brutal repercussions for the Chinese people, especially in Nanking. In 1940 they occupied or invaded part of northern French Indochina and later southern Indochina which included North and South Vietnam, Cambodia, Laos, Malaya (later called the Malay Peninsula), Thailand and Burma (later Myanmar).

The United States and other nations diplomatically protested these excursions but to no avail. Japan had no oil and very few other materials, like rubber, which were needed to supply a war machine. In 1941 the United States, Britain and the Netherlands placed an oil embargo on shipments to Japan and froze other assets, forcing Japan to look to the oil-rich fields of the Dutch East Indies (now Indonesia) for an oil supply. Japan's master plan to overcome this embargo included a massive strike on Pearl Harbor to neutralize the American fleet from hampering their shipping and expansionist plans in East Asia. The people in this country had previously remained resistant to any further involvement in wars but when Japan struck Pearl Harbor, December 7, 1941, everything changed. Over three thousand, five hundred Americans were killed or wounded, twenty warships were sunk or damaged including all eight battleships in the Pacific fleet in anchor at Pearl. Simultaneously Japan struck United States bases in Midway, Guam and the Philippines. The U.S. Navy had been severely crippled. Our aircraft carriers were spared because they were at sea but essentially our naval defenses were decimated.

Some analysts take the position that the U.S. forced Japan to go to war and Pearl Harbor, and all the horrors of war that took place later, could have been avoided if we had not placed an oil embargo on Japan. That's a preposterous analysis. Japan and Germany were determined to expand their empires regardless of the cost or consequences and no country could have stopped them short of war.

Signs of the inevitable world conflict were obvious all during the 1930s, not unlike the signs today. As early as 1934 news reports in papers such as the *New York Times* warned of these possibilities. In one month alone, February of 1934, a headline in the *Times* that read "Japan's Navy Held Too Big a Burden" quoted a Japanese foreign minister pointing out "that armaments were absorbing 40 percent of the (Japanese) national expenditure." Another article in that same month quoted a Russian Commissar who said, "It is now clear to all that Japan was the first nation to seek to issue from the depression by the aid of war. She has become the greatest purchaser of war material and of war industrial supplies in the world market, and is simultaneously carrying on the political preparation of the country for a more serious war than she waged in China. That is clear to the non-militarist eye." He continued, later in the article, "Our measures of self-defense seem to be an affront to the Japanese. Doubtless it would be preferable to our neighbors if we left our frontier in the same defenseless state as the Chinese Manchurian frontier in 1931. But that favor, in all politeness, we grant to no one."

Illustrative of the "ignore the problem and it will go away" philosophy of the United States at that time is a paragraph in a marvelous book, *Footprints in Courage*, published in 2002 by Badger Books, Inc., Oregon, WI. The author, Kristin Gilpatrick, tells the story of Alf Larson of Crystal, MN, a survivor of the World War II Bataan Death March. Mr. Larson enlisted in the U.S. Army Air Corps in 1939 and was on duty in the Philipine Islands later that year. He experienced first hand the lack of readiness of our military in that part of the world. After the attack on Pearl Harbor the Japanese invaded the Philipines with a vengeance.

U.S. troops, with gallant assistance from Philipine forces, were ill-equipped to stop them. In *Footprints in Courage*, Mr. Larson says (on page 25), " The armament we had consisted of old World War I Lewis anti-aircraft guns, the ones with the drum on top of them, and they would jam up! Everything we had over there was World War I stuff, including many rifles. The first airplane ride I took over there was in a ZB3 where the pilot sat in front, the gunner sat in back and everything was open. We were that outdated. The Japanese zeros could fly circles around everything we had over there at that time."

Mr. Larson continues, "American knew, should have known, war was coming, but we weren't ready. Some of the P-40 fighters we had didn't have any cooling fluid because it hadn't been shipped with the dang things! So, there they sat. A lot of them were destroyed on the ground because they couldn't take off without cooling fluid."

Captured by the Japanese in May 1942, after U.S. troops made their final stand on Corregidor, Mr. Larson was one of eight thousand U.S. troops, already in pitiful condition, forced to march eighty miles with well-nigh no food or water in what has appropriately been called the Bataan Death March. Almost half the troops either perished or were brutally slain along the way in violation of every known tenet of the Geneva Convention. Mr. Larson remained a prisoner of war in Japan until September 1945. His book (available from bookstores, $14.95) is a must-read for anyone interested in that period in our history and highly recommended for those who want an accurate account of those terrible days.

On the European front, where Hitler was reigning supreme in Germany, an article in the *Times,* on February 4, 1934, by special correspondence from Berlin, was headlined "ARMING BY REICH HELD INEVITABLE." The subheading read, "If demands are denied it is asserted Germany will proceed in secret, Reserve forces large, Potential army is estimated in millions and plants are at high efficiency." The article explained those headlines with these chilling details: "There can be no doubt of her (Germany's) intention. The remarkable intensification and improvement in the methods of training, disciplining, controlling, uniforming and organizing manpower since National Socialism came to power have surprised even close observers. What will rearmed Germany do? Her leaders claim that, with the open acknowledgement and open attainment of her right to practical equality in armaments, the sense of grievance will disappear, that there will be a better hope of lasting peace in Europe than ever before. Her uneasy neighbors recall that Germany also has territorial claims, and ask whether the sense of grievance in a Germany rearmed would not simply transfer itself to these."

In another section of the paper the *Times* displayed a map of Europe with the headline "Austrian Drama Approaches" and the caption beneath the map reading "The Nazi Shadow Over Europe. The shaded areas on the map indicate those countries which are threatened by the spread of Hitlerism, Austria immediately, and Hungary, Czechoslovakia and Yugoslavia if Austria comes under Nazi influence." This map was about fifty percent shaded. It should have been obvious to the reader of the *Times*, that the Nazi's "shadow" was fast enveloping all of Europe. It is doubtful the *New York Times* was the only paper in the United States reporting these trends. And this was 1934, seven years before Pearl Harbor!

In the years that followed, 1942 to 1945, both countries, Japan and Germany, were soundly defeated by the United States and its allies but at horrific cost in life and casualties to every nation involved. The U.S. turned from its isolationist stance of the 1930s to a full war effort. Women took over much of the production responsibility for war materiel and domestic products and services, sixteen million men (and some women) were mobilized in the armed forces and this country "went to war" in the full sense of the term. Horror stories of treatment of our captured military personnel abounded, particularly in the Pacific area. Life at home for civilians was difficult. These were years in the lives of everyone in the country that will never be forgotten.

This is the reason people living today, soldier or civilian, who went through that period, feel so passionate about those years. As a teen of seventeen in 1941 I couldn't wait to enlist in the Navy after Pearl Harbor and be off to training camp at Great Lakes Naval Training Center in December, 1941. Now that period is slipping from memory and certainly from the history books in high school and college. This oversight is an affront to all those who suffered through that War, civilians and military alike.

Sometimes war is the only solution. It's the last solution but not one to avoid at the prospect of terrorism or enslavement when inflicted on peace loving, compassionate, reasonable people. Are wars the worst of all solutions? I don't believe they are. In 2002, in a story by the Associated Press, dated October 4, the World Health Organization, in a meeting in Geneva, reported an estimated 1.6 million people worldwide met premature and violent deaths in the year 2000. 815,000 of this total killed themselves, 520,000 were murdered and 310,000 died in wars. The report added, "For every person who died, twenty to forty others were hospitalized with injuries." It appears war is not our greatest evil!

Are there lessons to be learned from the Great Depression days? Yes, there are. Ignoring dangers in the world, pretending they don't exist, does not insure peace. We had no choice but war in 1941 after the attack on Pearl Harbor. We may not have choices in the years ahead. We should not be afraid to go to war when that is the only logical option to preserve the safety of our citizens and the security of our country.

◆ Chapter Three: **EDUCATION**

Education may provide the most striking contrast between the world today and the world of the 1930s, the Great Depression period.

My high school years were rich with cultural subjects as the previous chapters outlined. I received average grades (I should have studied more) but, nevertheless, enjoyed those high school years because learning was the dominant purpose. There were no diversity or sex classes and no discipline problems to interfere with our learning. There was an emphasis on history, particularly American history, and languages. There was an emphasis on the great conflicts (wars) of history and the explorations that led to the discovery and settlement of the United States. Western civilization was hailed as a positive force in world affairs, not a corrupt influence on our society as presently portrayed.

I am repelled at many of the subjects my children and grandchildren are forced to endure in today's high schools. The emphasis seems to be on getting along and vocational style training. Students should learn how to operate a computer terminal on their own time or on the job. High school need not teach how to conduct oneself in a job interview or manage a checkbook. The result has been students who can't do arithmetic except on a calculator, can't write a letter without embarrassing grammatical errors, have handwriting that is undecipherable and can't speak clearly enough to be understood.

But the major contrast is in higher education. My college classes were graded on the curve. A certain percentage of students received an A, a larger percentage a B, most students a C, fewer a D and fewer still an F. The emphasis was on study. Polities were confined to classes with those subjects paramount to their mission. History, philosophy, even the classics, were emphasized along with one's major, of course.

There was a civility and respect for institutions of higher learning and the professors and administrators that ran them. Athletics were campus oriented and the college teams were held in high esteem. A college graduate of the 1930s and 1940s received a well-rounded education with a respect for learning and our history.

The environment on college campuses today is in stark contrast. Political correctness is the dominant theme. Dissent is squelched unless a viewpoint is antagonistic to historic American ideals. Dissent is applauded for the dissenters but dissent of dissent is not permitted. The curriculum is loaded with courses on the evils of Western civilization and the subjugation of minorities, women and criminals. Professors are rarely seen in the classroom and many universities have turned into research departments in search of ever-increasing federal funding. The primary purpose of an education should be to teach students how to think, how to solve problems, not what to think. Students should be educated after four years, not just trained.

The culprit is the federal funding on which all colleges and universities have become dependent and an elitist attitude that highly educated persons know what is best for all of society. It's not too strong a statement that the prevailing political philosophy in higher education today is socialistic. There is a demeaning and demonic attitude to the capitalist system. Socialistic systems where the government takes responsibility (and control) of a citizen's life from cradle to grave are favored and promoted.

This is tragic. Students graduate from some of our most prestigious colleges believing a capitalist system is evil and their parents, who probably hold fundamental values of thrift and honesty, are dupes no longer worthy of their respect. A concurrent theme of this latest modernism is no place for right and wrong, no absolutes, no standards. No one should be judgmental. Everyone has the right to do what feels good. What hypocrisy! In a true socialistic system, only the ruling elite have any rights. The proletariat are slaves in rights if not in name. The expectation that socialistic principles and a non-judgmental philosophy can co-exist is ludicrous, of course, but the desire to denigrate and vilify capitalism is so strong as to negate reason.

This evolves from decades-old social and political bias in colleges and universities. Dozens of articles and books have reported that ninety percent of the professors in these schools favor and vote for just one philosophy and one political party. A noted columnist recently reported that at one prominent Eastern college, where party affiliation could be determined, fifty-four professors voted for one of the major political parties and three voted for the other major party. That degree of bias does not, by any stretch of the imagination, result in students obtaining an unbiased education at the very period in their lives where they should be given the history and the facts on which to make informed decisions that will shape their future.

In fact, this degree of prejudice in our schools is doing more than shortchanging students in the education they are receiving. It's dishonest, tragic and repulsive for all of these students and, even more importantly, the long-range future of the country. It's difficult for me to understand how top administrators at these schools can allow this situation to persist. A litmus test for professors is not recommended but some better balance than fifty-four to three could be easily achieved without harming "academic freedom" or injuring anyone's tender sensibilities.

More ominously, what this suggests is this bias was achieved purposely by the administrators. It is not an accident. That is the most foreboding aspect of this meltdown in educational integrity.

If we have any concern for the truth in this country, for our long-range welfare, how can our top educational administrators, much less the general populous, allow this prejudice to exist? I'm tempted to invoke the name of a revered deity here to emphasize my point but will refrain from such invocation in deference to the aversion of those same administrators for anything religious.

I don't believe anything highlights the degradation of today's educational system as succinctly as the trend in colleges to peace studies programs. It is reported that over one hundred colleges offer a degree in these programs, often called "Peacemaking" or some variation thereof. The majority of these one hundred colleges offer masters and doctorate degrees in this subject. One might ask the simple-minded question, "Where are the programs for making war? If there are some just wars, don't we need some majors in "warmaking?" The "analogy" illustrates the absurdity.

After graduation with a bachelor degree in "peacemaking" I wonder what line of work that student would seek? That should test the mettle of a college recruiter!

In all seriousness, activism on a college campus as an adjunct to an education in law, literature, teaching, the sciences or whatever, is to be applauded. There is also nothing wrong with a light sprinkling of courses on the subject over a four-year period but carrying only courses on peacemaking as one's major for four years is a farce.

The parents who pay for this "education" are suckers. That's a plebeian word but no word is more appropriate. College administrators who devise and sanction these programs deserve even harsher condemnation for their efforts.

A longtime peace activist, coincidentally employed on the faculty of one of these programs, was reported saying, "These kids are already on the path when they come to me. [They] are coming faster to their radicalism then we ever did. Look out." Indeed we should!

So what have these trends achieved in today's culture? It may not be too far fetched to point to a large group of graduates adept at binge drinking. The tragedy is so many young people have had the opportunity for a college education, but too high a percentage have only learned to despise Western civilization and the foundations of a free and equal society envisioned by our founding fathers. Our most precious commodity, the real and basic freedom of the individual citizen, has been tossed aside in a morass of regulations and restrictions that no one who created the Constitution of the United States of America anticipated.

It would be easy to go on outlining statistics of the problems of today's education system but I promised not to do that in this book. Numerous polls, however, have shown that high school graduates cannot answer simple questions like, "What is the name of the vice-president of the country?" or "What war was begun by Pearl Harbor?"

A poll taken by the National Geographic – Roper 2002 Global Literacy Survey and reported in an article by Andres Oppenheimer, distributed by Knight Ridder News Service, and reprinted in the *St. Paul Pioneer Press* newspaper on December 3, 2002, reviewed some amazing results from young adults aged 18 to 24 in the United States. "Fifty-eight percent of young Americans could not locate Japan (on a map), 65 percent couldn't locate France and 69 percent couldn't locate the United Kingdom. About 11 percent of the young Americans couldn't even locate the United States on the map. By comparison, the poll found higher levels of geographic knowledge in Sweden, Germany, Italy, France, Japan, Canada and Great Britain. Only Mexico...scored lower." The article closes with, "Perhaps, the next time the United Nations holds a summit on education, it should include some funding to help teach geography to young Americans."

Another recent indication of the general deterioration in education is from an Associated Press report in March 2003, on the subject of understanding instructions for the use of car seats. The report states, "Instructions for installing child car seats are written in language too difficult for many adults to understand, researchers say. Such manuals are written at a tenth-grade reading level on average...while data suggest that nearly a quarter of U.S. adults read at or below a fifth-grade level." The article continues, "Reading difficulty was tied to the number of words with three or more syllables appearing in 10-sentence samples."

So words with three or more syllables are difficult for over a quarter of U.S. adults to understand? That's pathetic. If that doesn't rouse us from our educational stupor, I don't know what will.

Suffice to say, education is our major crisis today and unless we find a way to correct it, the future of this great country is dim indeed. An enormous first step would be to encourage parents to become a part of school activities. Specifically, allow them to visit the schoolroom of their son or daughter at any time without restriction, no advance notice. Most if not all schools prohibit parents, in part, at least, from visiting the classroom without prior notice of several hours or days. The reason for this is teachers and administrators are attempting to conceal what and how they are teaching. This practice is indefensible. It is well known that wherever parents take an active interest, the students do better work. Parents must be encouraged to attend and participate. If they don't agree with some aspect of the instructions, that should be discussed at an appropriate time.

Excuses for security reasons are not valid. Security can be maintained at the perimeter of a school, if it is necessary, but once identified and cleared parents should have open access. Anything less is simply an attempt to hide teaching practices.

The constant cry – no, howl – today is for more money. This was rarely discussed in the 1930s. Schools consisted of teachers teaching in the classroom, an assistant principal, the principal and maybe two or more record-keeping clerks, depending on the size of the school. In today's school, "administration" has taken on a concept all its own rivaling the size of the teacher corps. Only those endowed with mystical powers of conjecture can surmise what all these administrators do. The result is public school spending in this country now averages seven thousand dollars per year per pupil with several Eastern states at a ten thousand dollar level. Public school funding is obscene in comparison to the results it achieves. Salient innovations are coeducational dormitories, whether sodas should be removed from the lunchroom and left-tilted campus newspapers that make *Izvestia* and *Pravda* resemble the Magna Charta.

Cheating is the rule, not the exception. Articles have documented examples where seventy-five percent cheat in a test. If a student is disciplined or – horrors – expelled for this practice, parents protest en masse or sue the school board for re-entry and damages to the student's fragile psyche. The attitude, by students and parents alike, is "everybody does it. What's the big deal?" That's a very inappropriate measurement to apply to any problem. No, not just inappropriate. It's dangerous, foolhardy and destructive on a long-term basis to any thinking, deliberative society.

Plagiarism, an obvious form of cheating, is on the rise. The culprit here is the Internet. For a few dollars–or for free–a report on any book, subject or person is available. But this practice can be squelched if schools go after it aggressively. The *Hastings Star Gazette* (You haven't heard of Hastings, Minnesota? Too bad. It's a lovely town), reported in an article in its November 21, 2002 paper, that the key is to have a written policy disseminated to all students. The article, by the *Star Gazette* managing editor, illustrates the success in halting plagiarism at Hastings High School. The English

Department in this school has had a written policy against it for years. This has worked so well the other departments have decided to adopt it. It defines plagiarism as, " take and use as one's own thoughts, writings, etc., of another, take and use (a passage, plot, etc.) from the work of another writer and represent it as one's own. Plagiarism means writing facts, quotations or opinions that you got from someone else or from books, articles, movies, television, tapes, speeches or the Internet without identifying your source. Plagiarize means to 'kidnap' ideas thought up and written down by someone else. It is a form of stealing." The policy statement goes on to advise, "Penalties for plagiarism can be severe; failure and removal from the course will be enforced if caught cheating. Unintentional plagiarism is still plagiarism, so be careful and know the rules."

This policy is placed in every student's handbook at the beginning of the school year. The student must sign it and have his parents or guardian sign it. One smart aleck student was quoted as saying, "I heard some [students] forged their parents' signatures on the plagiarism form." That practice is discounted as prevalent, however, and this school, in the small town of Hastings, population twenty thousand, just a few miles southeast of the Minneapolis-St. Paul metropolitan area, is to be commended and applauded for having a written policy on this form of cheating and doing its best to eliminate it.

It is evident what has led us to this miserable situation and the difficulties in correcting it. Public education has become a monolithic monster with a half-trillion dollar appetite and no one in control. It's run for benefit of the monster, not the students. If you doubt this, listen to some of our highest-paid sports heroes, most of them reportedly with a college education, being interviewed. Their responses are undecipherable.

Myriad solutions are necessary. Unfortunately, there is no political will to change school structure legislatively. They will only change if they are forced to change, i.e., by competition. This will not happen until substantial vouchers are available from some source so students can go to other schools. The old canard that public funding is required to cover the extra expenses for disadvantaged or recalcitrant students is false. Examples abound where private schools have taken on hoards of poorly performing students and elevated them to

45

excellence by challenging them and disciplining them. Public education must "fear for its life" before it will change any of its failing practices.

The other falsehood, that public money shouldn't go to schools with a religious affiliation, is not even supported by an honest reading of the Constitution of the United States. But more about that will be discussed in the government section of this book.

After vouchers are firmly established and half the students have transferred to non-public schools, the curriculum must do a one-eighty and start teaching history and the classics. I remember in my youth going to a public library and gazing in awe at all the books on the shelf with elaborate lettering and thick binding and names like Socrates, Homer, Caesar, Rousseau, Shakespeare and, yes, even George Washington and Thomas Jefferson, much as that might shock the history revisionists of today. Those writers will challenge young minds and open them to a realization that all the evils of twenty-first century society are not the fault of our European ancestors, more succinctly "dead white males," but a failure of our educational system to educate and produce scholars rather than train robots.

History and the classics teach, challenge and inspire all at the same time. Readers would learn, among other lessons, that history is replete with just wars and evil wars. That was the history of ancient Greece, a country whose society and civilization the United States mirrors today. Our World Wars I and II were just wars. GIs on the beaches of Iwo Jima and Okinawa, and on Normandy, to name just a few invasions, gave their lives in a just war. The world had no other choice but to fight that imperialism and it has no other choice today in fighting terrorism. The United States is not hated because it is evil. It is hated because it is a successful democracy, its citizens are free and prosperous. Autocratic despots in the world cannot tolerate those examples if they hope to hold onto their own evil authorities.

The elitists in our colleges and universities today, if they would study the classics, would be able to differentiate between just wars and evil wars and cease beating their breasts about the superiority of conciliation, negotiation and co-existing with tyrants and oppressors who wish either to subjugate us or kill us, whichever is quicker and easier for them. Studying ancient Greece, or the history of many other old civilizations, would illuminate those lessons for our young people so they might think differently from their elitist professors.

Next in importance is religious study. The United States is a Christian-based, Christian-oriented culture and it should remain so. There should be no penalty nor discrimination against other religions but this country was founded on Christian principles and we should never stray from that heritage. It is not our responsibility to promote other cultures or religions. It is equally incumbent on those cultures and religions to learn to co-exist with the Christian environment and the teachings of this country since the days when the Pilgrims landed on Plymouth Rock. Religious study gives students examples of absolutes: You shouldn't do this or that. It sets standards, a scary phrase to many today. It gives examples of all these and offers a path for both personal and civil peace that is unparalleled from any other teaching.

Today even churches are becoming afraid to provide moral leadership. They fear their membership will drop if they "tell people how to live." That's an actual quote I heard recently from a member of clergy. How sad! If young people aren't taught "how to live," what are they to be taught? How not to live?

The fear of connecting any aspect of religion to public education is so irrational it has taken on unbelievable dimensions. The Christian Bible is based on the golden rule, "Do unto others as you would have them do unto you," or, to quote directly from the Bible, Mathew 7:12 (Christian Community Bible, Copyright © Bernardo Hurault 1994), "So, do to others whatever you would that others do to you: there you have the Law and the Prophets." I find it difficult to be afraid, suspicious, or have any misgivings, about an objective as well-meaning and forthright as that.

We didn't question "religion in the schools" in the 1930s and 1940s. We said the Pledge of Allegiance every day before class, recited the Ten Commandments whenever appropriate and God and religion were mentioned frequently in the normal course of study. We certainly did not worry about the religious connotations of holiday observances such as Christmas, Thanksgiving, Easter, Holy Week and similar days that send 2003 irreligious activists into frenzy. There are schools today that will not allow the term "Christmas" to be used. Instead of "Merry Christmas" one can only say "Season's Greetings" or "Happy Holidays." Do we realize the connotations this has for the morality of this country, without which no country can long exist?

Another change, sorely needed, is the cessation of overemphasis, particularly at the college level, on athletics. Athletics should be an extra-curricular activity equal but not greater in emphasis than the student newspaper, debating club, band or other volunteer activity. It's no coincidence that more scandals arise in colleges from overemphasis on athletics than any other activity, in or out of the classroom. Some colleges have one scandal after the other, are consumed by the success or failure of their football team and place their football coach on a higher pedestal than the president of the school. This practice might have some justification if it added to the learning process but the opposite is usually the result.

We need to get a grip on college athletics in this country and throttle it back to a proper perspective before it consumes the entire educational process ala a dinosaur consuming a rabbit. In my youth we revered the college athlete as sacrificing their time for their school and an example of the most virtuous part of the student body.

But in our efforts to improve the educational process in this country all changes pale in relation to the importance of parents in the school activities of their children. And we are not talking about yelling and screaming at the hockey game or berating the football coach. We are talking about parents visiting the school classroom frequently, talking to the teacher, examining the books their children are required to study, helping them, particularly in the lower grades, with their studies and, in the main, just staying INVOLVED, INVOLVED, INVOLVED with everything in school from kindergarten to the senior year.

There is no substitute for this parental care and oversight. The majority of teachers, the staunchest proponents of the status quo, will agree. It's far more important than funding. Funding is almost irrelevant. There are countless examples of excellent schools that have funding less than a fourth of schools academically inferior.

When my stepmother or other members of her family slacked off their oversight of my schoolwork, I slacked off and my grades fell accordingly. When they followed, cajoled and inquired about what I was doing, my grades, and more importantly my learning, increased. Constant parental oversight is a simple solution to many of our educational woes, but simple solutions have never been very effective because they are easy to overlook.

It's easy, obviously, to blame all our educational problems on the school system but parents share a substantial percentage of the blame. Students are being sent to school with no training or discipline from home and once in school the parents ignore their problems unless the police appear at their door. This is unfair to the schools and a guaranteed recipe for failure for the students.

We are in trouble. It would not be unfair to blame our current problems in this society on the education our young people have received since the 1960s. That generation is now adults and they are bringing up another generation of grade school, teen and college students. If we do not favor increased promiscuity, declining morals, loss of patriotism, a growing aversion to religion and indifference to cheating and lower test scores, we have only a declining educational system to blame and the acquiescence of compliant parents.

Immediately an entire legion of parents will say, "The schools in my district are good, very good. What are you talking about?" Fortunately there are millions of students receiving good educations but the problem is the "average" student. Millions of those are not receiving a quality, balanced education. The country operates on the skill and intelligence of all its citizens, not only those fortunate ones who were lucky enough to have good teachers and wise administrators. It's difficult when you discuss this subject with a truly excellent teacher. He or she takes umbrage at this charge of incompetence, and I sympathize with them, but we all need to look at this as an industry, not one individual. Most at risk are the poorest schools in the poorest communities where discipline is the primary problem. Graduation rates are abysmal and education marginal or less. Then there is a large middle group where some teachers (not all, but a significant number) are putting out minimum effort and going along with textbooks and courses that are anti-American, anti-history, anti-capitalistic, irreligious, pro-multicultural, pro-feel good philosophy and allowing students to graduate with skills so low and attitudes so antagonistic no employer wants to hire them.

Cost is another problem. The appetite of educational systems for increased funding is ongoing and insatiable while the country's resources are diminishing. Primary in this dilemma is the burden of attempting to please every diversity idea that arises. My grandparents came to this country as immigrants with no knowledge of English or the customs and nuances of a strange land. They learned on the job and prospered in the main. Now we feel it essential to immediately provide the full training and benefits to all immigrants enjoyed by citizens who have lived here for decades.

An example is an article in the Minneapolis *Star Tribune* newspaper on December 17, 2002, by a staff writer, titled "Translations reflect Minnesota's changing population." It's reported in the article that "Application forms and telephone lines for the state Department of Human Services have been set up in 10 languages other than English: Arabic, Khmer, Croatian, Hmong, Lao, Oromo, Russian, Somali, Spanish and Vietnamese." In another part of the article relating to the school system, "Most forms for field trips, lunch subsidies and health information are translated into the district's top nine languages which also include Tibetan, Vietnamese, Khmer (Cambodian), Lao and the east African tongues Amharic and Oromo." Additionally, the article states, "The [Hennepin County Medical Center] is required by federal law to provide patients with an interpreter free of charge. About 60 interpreters who speak more than 15 languages are on staff, [a representative] said." Make no mistake. The funds for these programs are all coming from local, county, state or federal taxpayers.

Readers will note, by the way, that in the above citation from the Minneapolis *Star Tribune,* and in several subsequent citations in this book, " Minneapolis" is not italicized. The name of the paper is the *Star Tribune* and does not include "Minneapolis" despite the paper's long history, identity and location in that city. Without "Minneapolis," however, out-of-state readers would have no perspective on the location of the paper so I have taken the liberty of including that designation before the name.

Assimilation, to a degree, is a worthy goal but how much is proper? My grandparents received no assimilation assistance. In fact, immigrant children in school in those pioneer days regularly had fun poked at them for their different speech and dress. I also wonder how much assistance immigrants from this country would receive in the majority of foreign lands? Very little, I fear, despite the generosity of the United States in protecting and funding half the world with the necessities of life and tranquility when they land on our shores.

These are the problems our present educational system present. The danger to our country should be obvious. A country rarely disintegrates from outside threats. It goes to war and repels them. Rot and decay from within are not so easily overcome because they occur slowly over time and are difficult (almost impossible) to change without a cataclysmic event.

The nature of education is not likely to suffer an event of these proportions. Consequently, the only possibility for meaningful change is for the citizenry to finally get so fed up with the anti-everything higher education is teaching that a groundswell of public opinion develops and permeates upward to the politicians. This also must coincide with election of a president of the country who comprehends this problem and has the leadership capabilities to change it rather than exacerbate it by simply throwing more and more money at the problem.

A likely scenario? No, but possible. Let us all hope – and work – for that possibility. We may not have much time if public education is to be saved. An article in the Minneapolis *Star Tribune* on September 22, 2002, by James Walsh, staff writer, reported, "about one in ten of Minnesota's K-12 students (now) attend private schools, according to the 2000 census." The article goes on to report the percentage is higher in St. Cloud and St. Paul, hardly bastions of rich suburbanites. The percentages there are 20.8 and 15.4 percent respectively. These percentages exist despite the cost of "average annual tuition (for the private schools) ranging from $1,650 for kindergarten to $4,200 for the twelfth grade."

Education has always positioned itself as too important to be challenged. Question it and you are against children. This attitude has a long history. Even in the mid-1930s, in the depths of depression, with money scarce to non-existent, the following lead editorial appeared in the *Minneapolis Tribune* (the name of the paper at that time), headed "The Legislators and the Schools." It read, "The legislators who are eyeing the so-called 'fads and frills' in the schools of the state with a view to forcing a reduction in them are flirting around a hornet's nest. There are tens of thousands of estimable Minnesotans who resent nothing more bitterly than the suggestion that any part of the school dollar is being spent for non-essentials. As a matter of fact, they suspect that anyone who does not resent that suggestion is an implacable enemy of education, and would as soon as not doom the children of the state to a life of illiteracy and ignorance. To them, every move for economy is a move for destruction, and every demand for retrenchment a demand for the curtailment of the legitimate and proper functions of the schools.

"This attitude has not been softened by the difficulties which the schools have experienced in the depression; if anything, it has grown more rigid and unbending as unwelcome economies have been forced upon our educational systems. It therefore behooves those who would currently indict the schools of the state for their wasteful fads and fripperies to move with caution. It will not do to refer, in vague and nebulous terms, to the educational extravagances which must be abandoned in the interests of the taxpayers. The notion that all school expenditures are good, and therefore beyond criticism, is too firmly established for that."

Apparently hyperbole is always in vogue when discussing education.

I remember when I was young, I thought of college as something very special, a privilege granted to only a few, probably an unrealistic attainment for me. Now we are promoting it as a "right" of all young people. It's not a "right." Some can't handle it, others don't want it and should not be pushed into it. That's part of the same averaging problem again. Don't try and educate everyone beyond everyone's ability. It's a waste of time and counter-productive for the young person. Higher education should not be taken for granted. It should be available only to those who want it and are willing to work hard to achieve its benefits.

College should also not be a paper mill where forty-percent get As and forty-percent get Bs while taking a high percentage of multicultural, multi-social courses equipping them only to feel dissatisfied with everything in their lives and all their surroundings. Indicative of this laissez faire attitude in education, that is leading to awarding all students As and Bs, is a study from the American Council on Education (ACE) reported by the Associated Press in January 2003. The survey compiled data from over 250,000 students and over 400 colleges. The results showed forty-five percent of incoming college freshmen said they graduated from high school with an A average. The next largest group received Bs. "The C-grade is almost a thing of the past," a spokesperson for the ACE said. That's called grade inflation by any measurement!

Equally revealing in this survey was the admission from these college freshmen that when they were in high school, sixteen percent maintained their high averages by studying less than one hour per week. Only thirty-three percent said they studied more than six hours per week to maintain those high averages. That's just slightly over one hour per day! In other words students are getting higher grades for doing less. Is there any other conclusion? What's all this hoopla about being so busy in high school, so pressured, so challenged, there is no time for other activities?

Once enrolled in college, grades of As and Bs seem to be the norm. That's ridiculous. How can anyone compare a college transcript today with college grades of a decade or more ago? They can't, not with any relevancy. I've even heard professors justify this grade creep (I call it grade degradation) on parents who pay big money to send their son or daughter to college and expect the college to reward that support with a high grade for their offspring.

Is it too much to point out that somewhere, sometime, someone must act on principle less we all sink into a moralless quagmire?

Too many young people are being cheated by this type of education when they desperately need lessons from people who have gone before them, are wiser than they are and need facts upon which to decide the course of their own lives and make important decisions. They should not be cheated by an easy-going atmosphere that leaves them unchallenged and unhappy.

Students in high school, or eighteen- to twenty-two-year-olds in college, do not have all the answers. They should not be leading the revolt. They should be studying history and our world, seeking answers from wise men and women who have preceded them and learning how to make decisions for themselves to enhance their lives after school. That's key: Higher education should be a process of learning how to make a decision, not training per se, with the obvious exceptions, of course, of medicine, engineering, etc.

Yes, today's youth will be the world of tomorrow but I'm not confident we're educating young people and leaders for that future.

Rather, I believe we're slipping downward and this is unquestionably the most serious challenge this country faces.

Are there lessons to be learned from the Great Depression days? Yes, there are. We need to return to teaching more relevant subjects, by more unprejudiced professionals, in a disciplined environment, to students who really want to learn and leave out all the irrelevancy that is clouding and misdirecting our educational system today.

◆ Chapter Four: **FAMILY**

A difficult subject to discuss. There are similarities between the 1930s and today but major differences. The makeup of the family is one of these. I do not maintain a mother and father are indispensable in all families. Many single mothers and a few single fathers raise remarkable children. The point is the combination of a mother and father is preferred to a single parent. It's less stressful for the parent and the opportunity for successful parenting is increased. I did not have a conventional family but I did have a family that provided all the love and attention I needed.

By some standards, in fact, I had just a single parent, my stepmother, but I also had the advantage of other adults in the household who doubled as sisters, brother and father. At any rate, I never felt deprived of love in any way and looking back on those years I believe I may even have matured more quickly for lack of a conventional family structure. Everyone gets uptight when an unconventional family structure is assailed so we need to remember any organization can and does work if love and care are present.

Lest we forget, however, the purpose of this book is to compare today's world with the 1930s and 1940s. In 1930 few women held jobs. Magazine ads concentrated on what wives could do to make their husbands happy. Typical headlines read "If you want your husband to rave about your cooking, serve him (the latest food) tonight," or, "I won't stay in this house another minute! The big brute – complaining that his shirts are full of tattle-tale gray…after I've simply slaved over them," with a picture at the top of the ad of a man and woman, backs to each other, scowling. Then, in the bottom of the ad, the same couple is shown in each other's arms with the caption "What a lot I've learned in two short weeks! Look at him today…all kisses and smiles because his shirts are so nice and white. Mother was right. There's nothing like (the latest) soap for getting rid of tattle-tale gray that shows clothes aren't really clean."

Laugh, as you might, at these stereotypes, they represented a stable, nurturing family environment that produced a generation of people that conquered a severe depression and successfully fought World War II with love of family and patriotism their rallying cry.

Babies were also not neglected in advertising. It seemed cod liver oil was the secret to healthy ones. A prominent ad associated this amazing elixir with a "well-shaped head, fine full chest, strong back, straight legs and sound even teeth." Quite an endorsement!

All was not primitive, either, in the food preparation system. Numerous electric cooking devices were gaining acceptance (if one had some money) such as electric coffee makers, toasters and cooking ranges.

My stepmother was typical of the 1930s woman. She was at home to take care of her son and daughters and, in later years, me. But she was not a stranger to working outside the home. For several years prior to my birth, my stepmother and her husband owned and published a small-town weekly newspaper in Southern Minnesota. She assisted her husband in the newspaper office and would have continued this job if her husband had not died when I was one-year-old.

Even in the old days, which today's feminists so eagerly love to criticize, women could and did do both jobs, a housewife and work outside the home. The majority, nevertheless, were stay-at-home housewives. Was this an advantage for the children? I don't believe any rational person can claim day care is advantageous to stay-at-home mother-care. That defies logic and I believe a huge advantage children, and our world of the 1930s, had going for them.

My stepmother was there in the morning to see me off to school after a nutritious breakfast and determine I was adequately clothed for a one-mile walk to school, often in below-zero weather. She was there again when I came home from school to ask what I did all day, look at my schoolwork and, yes, usually had baked those ubiquitous little cookies which I eagerly sampled.

All the women, or men, rarely, who aren't able to stay at home because of economic reasons or because they prefer the activity of working outside the home, are not to be criticized if they have good reasons for doing it. But it was certainly an advantage for me, and other children of that period, to have a "stay-at-home" mom. In two-thirds of today's households the mother has a full time job. If that outside job is not essential, they should give their child-rearing responsibility their first priority and remain at home or reach agreement with their husband to stay home while they work. It's a sacrifice but one that should be made. Here's another example of how statistics often tell a false story. Poll after poll has revealed day care children suffer some disadvantage ranging from minor to major effects. Finally a poll came out that claimed children in day care obtained a better upbringing than children with a mother at home. That's an absurd conclusion.

Another feature of family life in my time was a family together for dinner each evening. That's not a small advantage. Besides the nutritional advantage of a home-cooked meal versus a fast food menu, the main feature is family conversation. I was the only child in my family but I wasn't ignored at dinner. I was encouraged to talk about what I had been doing all day or any problems I had encountered. At the same time I listened to adult conversation and learned a great deal about current events and news from outside the home I would not otherwise have absorbed.

A negative feature was lack of space for everything we did. Houses were small, people doubled up in bedrooms, even, in fact, in the same bed. There were few playgrounds except adjacent to schools and few lawns of any size. We lived on a very noisy streetcar line but felt fortunate to have convenient transportation. Families did things together even if they were as simple as listening to the radio, going to church or visiting relatives. We were together in almost all activities, child or parent, young or old, male or female. That's a wonderful environment in which a growing child can feel safe, secure, loved and cherished. It's not duplicated today in too many families and, ultimately, society will suffer for this omission.

Maybe we're suffering now. A survey in the August 14, 2002 *Journal of the American Medical Association*, made to study the "Effect of Mandatory Parental Notification on Adolescent Girl's Use of Sexual Health Care Services," surveyed sexually active girls ages twelve to seventeen. That's right! TWELVE years of age. The survey found fifty-nine percent said they "would stop using all sexual health care services, delay testing or treatment for HIV or other STDs, or discontinue use of specific (but not all) sexual health care services if their parents were informed that they were seeking prescribed contraceptives." Additionally, the survey found ninety-nine percent of these girls who would stop going to the clinics "indicated that they would continue having sexual intercourse."

Obviously the definition of the word "family" is different today. They spend far less time together, talk less with each other, eat fewer meals with each other, and, if this survey is any indication, know less about what each member is doing including girls twelve years of age engaged in sexual intercourse outside the home. Unheard of in my world of the 1930s!

Differences in families are also conspicuous in the pictures they take. In the 1930s the emphasis was on people: after church on Sunday, going for a ride, students outside a school, sitting on the porch with friends or even a newborn foal following its mother. Today the emphasis is on events: a birthday party, a school play, a wedding, a graduation, maybe a hockey game.

This became evident to me recently when I was browsing an old picture album from my birth mother. Most of the album reflects the years from 1911 to 1918 when she was teaching school in remote areas of North Dakota and it is vivid with photographs of people, not events. The old black-and-white pictures are yellowing and fading now but the white-ink notations under them remain clear. I see, in her handwriting, beneath the photos, "school pupils at Stebbins," and "out for a good time." Then I read, "out on the farm," and "the dear old bridge near my old home," and "leaving home," and "comfortably resting after a hard day's study," and then "fond remembrances of happy days." Today's albums are unlikely to have any personal notations. Supposedly the picture tells all!

As I look through this old album, remembering my loss at never knowing my birth mother, a wonderful, unpretentious woman who died so I might live, I see those pictures of people doing simple things, but the things in life that really mattered to them. Families were sacrosanct in those years. They were the glue that held us together in troubled times. In our current helter-skelter, time-deprived social order, jobs and money come first, families and their activities often an afterthought. This is a tragedy for which we are paying dearly in the present decade.

My stepmother's son, who was twenty years older than me, and frequently filled the role of my father, was a good baseball player. He played in college but when I was one-year-old, his father (my step-guardian at the time) died and he had to quit school and assist in the small town newspaper business. That business was sold two years later because no one in the family had the expertise to keep it going and the son (actually my cousin) went to work to help support us all. We moved to Minneapolis and in the summers he played semi-pro baseball for a local team on Saturday afternoons. He took me to all the games and I sat on the bench with the players on his team. He was a "good field, no hit" shortstop, so he never progressed beyond semi-pro leagues, but I will never forget those Saturday afternoons, with nothing else to do in those difficult years and the stands full of people cheering for his team, and my anxiety for him each time he fielded a ball at shortstop or came to bat. His shoe size was the same as mine so after I came back from service in World War II, I used his baseball shoes and glove for twenty-five years playing on numerous fast pitch company softball teams.

It's the little things children remember of their lives which help them to raise their own children and we were rich in those family remembrances. I will always be grateful to this cousin for his admonishments to me against swearing. I would frequently be playing some kind of sport in the alley in back of our house and he would come home from work, park his car in the garage, and walk by our game. If I missed a catch or fumbled something, I might forget where I was and occasionally use a swear word. He would stop right there, say to me and all the boys around me, "I don't want you to swear, ever. Swearing is just a sign you don't have a better word to use. Do you understand what I'm saying?"

This practice of swearing provides another contrast between the two periods. It is casual and routine today but still offensive. I believe we were better off for its absence.

There is little doubt a breakdown of the family, wherever it occurs, is a primary cause of violent crime. The government would like us to believe material factors such as reduced job opportunities and insufficient funding for social programs is the cause but that's not accurate. We've spent trillions of dollars on these programs in the past few decades with little result. What is accurate is an alarming increase in teenage mothers, single-parent households, illegitimacy and violence in the schools. Violence breeds more violence and this is obvious not only in statistics but in the increasing friction in our society from young children who won't obey their parents to road rage on our highways perpetrated by adults who were never taught to respect the rights of others.

The latest phenomenon in the abuse category is parent abuse. You're acquainted with child abuse, partner (spouse) abuse and elder abuse. Now comes parent abuse and it's increasing. That's when children, especially teens, become violent to their parents. This abuse may be verbal (swearing or loud shouting) or it may be physical including the use of weapons. It's not a surprise to me. For the past decade or two I've watched pre-school to grade school children engage in tantrums and hit at their parents to get whatever they want – and they usually get it! Ten years later, when these children become teens, they employ the same successful techniques against their parents except now it becomes more serious and more violent. This trend shouldn't shock anyone. It's been observable for many years. The only surprise is how reluctant society has been to talk about it. Parents, in particular, hesitate to admit they can't control a son or daughter whatever their age.

The tragic aspect of parent abuse is there is no quick fix. Five-year-olds who manipulate will become fifteen-year-olds who swear and shout at their parents and/or threaten with physical abuse or with weapons.

Consider the behavior today in movie theaters. Loud laughter and loud, derisive comments about the movie are routine. People, usually teens, make and receive cell phone calls with the movie in progress. Someone in a newspaper comment column recently reported a teen in the front row was using their cell phone to call a friend several rows back. Is there any behavior today that is unacceptable? Apparently not.

It's a long evolutionary solution to these problems. Government agencies can't change them. Individual people, citizens, must change them.

Another recent phenomenon illustrating the difference in the 1930s and today is the pressure from women for unusual delivery room requests in the hospital. In the 1930s hospital rooms, for maternity or otherwise, were kept quiet and simple. Visitors were restricted to specific hours of the day and evening and often only two or three people were allowed in the room at one time. Visiting someone in the hospital was a rather solemn occasion with a lot of rules and regulations attached to it. Not so today! A *Wall Street Journal* article in December, 2002, by Elizabeth Bernstein, titled "Divas in the Delivery Room," reported birth mother's requests to make "placenta prints" to take home, have professional photographers snap the birth, birthday parties in the delivery room, and "letting one father be naked at the delivery." Another request was from a mother who "...instead of her midwife, she wanted someone else to do the actual delivery; her five-year-old daughter, ...dressed in her favorite Scooby-Doo sundress. 'I didn't want her to feel left out,'" said the mother. Questions of hygiene, sterilization and common sense aside, this marvel of comportment highlights eloquently the wide gap in the two eras.

There is an ongoing concern about increased immigration to this country. The long-term effect on all of us has many dimensions but one effect that should not be ignored is the propensity of the immigrants to have large families and their efforts to keep their families intact in all of their activities. Part of this is a natural inclination to group together and protect each other to avoid language and custom problems but they have found, in the countries from which they emigrated, probably poor and crime-ridden, that a tight knit family can offer protection to its members they cannot experience singly. We long-term citizens should learn from that lesson.

The modern, fragmented do-what-you-want style of today's family is no answer to solving numerous problems that arise as children grow and experience new challenges. The family of the 1930s was a more homogeneous unit. This was particularly true in farming areas. A lack of money and transportation contributed to this but the reasons run deeper. Mother and children were needed to provide labor on the farm. The mother frequently performed all the duties of a wife in those days (cooking, cleaning, sewing, first-line doctor) and then, after doing barnyard chores, went to the field to assist in haying, driving horses, herding cattle or anything else that needed doing. Children helped with all these chores, depending on their age, but no able-bodied member of the family escaped a portion of this hard work.

This kept the family together regardless of the intent. Because of the hardships of the depression, however, most young people were eager to leave this life at their earliest opportunity and those years were the beginning of a trend for them to leave rural areas and migrate to the cities. That trend has continued. In recent years there has been some migration back to rural life as cities have become increasingly crime-ridden and congested but to claim this trend as significant long-term is probably inaccurate. The longing is there, especially from anyone raised in the solitude and beauty of rural surroundings, but the pull of city life with its perceived advantages is usually too strong to allow much movement.

But look in any magazine or newspaper and count the stories about the mystique of going back to a simpler life. An example is the rather sudden prominence in recent years of the State of North Dakota, particularly here in Minnesota. Many Midwesterners have looked on North Dakota for decades as a barren, remote, treeless expanse of territory in which no one would want to live. Many of us know that is inaccurate. Eastern North Dakota, particularly the Red River Valley area, holds some of the richest, most fertile farmland in the country. The Western half is a combination of ranch land and majestic scenery.

Much of the negativism comes from people who lived in North Dakota during the Great Depression when drought, grasshoppers or other natural disasters routinely wiped out their crops. I talked recently to a person who grew up there in that period and said all during her teens she would sit outside on the broken down porch (they were too poor to buy lumber to fix it), look out at the dusty gravel road going by, and say to herself, "There must be a better life than this somewhere. I don't know where that road leads but one day I'm going to follow it out of here."

Nostalgia is only the surface reason for this longing to return, however. Our cities have become increasingly crowded, dirty, with intolerable commuting times and unrealistic prices. These factors lead to frustrations and breakup in the family and this motivates many people, and families, to move to rural areas.

A recent experience I had is illustrative of the value of ancestors and families. Several years ago, I decided to visit the cemetery in North Dakota where my paternal grandparents were buried. With age (I was then about seventy), I discovered, comes a longing to relive younger years but it's more than that. It's reaching out to your parents, grandparents and aunts and uncles, whom you may have overlooked in those early years, or at least did not talk to about events in their lives, that are now closed to you after they are deceased, and one feels a compulsion to fill in some of the blanks.

I know this sounds incredible, but never having lived with my father on the farm, I had not visited my paternal grandparent's graves since they died in the 1930s and my stepmother took me to their funerals. I wasn't certain of the location of the cemetery, but on a cold, windy day in November, with a North Dakota nor'wester brewing, and after visiting four or five cemeteries in the approximate area, I finally found where they were buried. From one hundred feet it was unrecognizable as a cemetery. Lilac bushes and other shrubs and brush had overgrown everything. Inside the cemetery numerous graves were sunken, covered by brush and weeds, or the footmarkers and gravestones cracked, broken, tipped over or missing. It was a desolate scene but one increasingly common in remote areas as people move away, burials cease, the adjacent church burns down or is removed and there are few or no one left who has an interest in those buried there.

I stood looking at these graves and wondered why two immigrants to this country in the mid-1850s, who homesteaded this desolate place, and struggled all their lives to eke out a living while raising an honest, hard-working family of eight children, should be ignored in death. I subsequently visited a number of farms in the neighborhood trying to learn if records for the cemetery were available. I believed I also had an uncle buried there. At the same time I wanted to see who might be interested in doing something to fix up the grounds.

It was discouraging. Most families now living in the area either had no one buried there or were too old to give any assistance. After that I talked to numerous bureaucrats in the township, the county and the State of North Dakota, and found sympathy, but reluctance to do anything or provide any funds for doing it. Luck intervened, however, and one of the families I visited had a relative who had moved away but was interested in restoring the cemetery. This woman and her husband, with the help of surrounding farmers who became motivated when they sensed some organization developing to clean this up, toiled for many days and weeks one summer in the hot North Dakota sun to identify unmarked graves, furnish markers, cut down brush, build a new fence and even install a new flag and flag pole.

The result was miraculous. The woman who led this restoration followed that feat with a two hundred-page book, self-published, detailing the effort. More importantly it details the history of pioneer families in that area gleaned from conversations with them and research of county and church records heretofore never studied. The title of this remarkable book, by Everett and Marlene Haibeck Vorthmann, is *Church at Four Corners,* in recognition of the location of the cemetery and the church adjacent to four counties.

One paragraph in this book by a resident tells a lot about those days. It reads, "Like all of our neighbors we were very poor, but as children we didn't know that. Our folks never talked about money, nor was it often visible. We wondered one Christmas though when we didn't get any gifts. Dad saw our stockings hanging here and there so he jokingly sneaked potatoes into our sox. Poor folks, maybe sadder for them than for us children. We didn't have Christmas trees for years because they didn't grow on the prairie. The congregation would send to Minneapolis for a community tree for church, then on Christmas day we would drive with horse and sleigh. We would have a few childish gifts and a picnic lunch for us and oats for the horses. After services everyone brought their picnic lunches into the pews. As it got darker the tree was lit with candles. We enjoyed the program, and everyone marched around the tree. It took three or more rings to include everyone. The candles had to be watched, because they often set the tree on fire. Several men of the congregation watched with long handled snuffers. Each child received a small brown bag filled with an apple or orange, peanuts in the shell, and hard candy, and that was a real treat. The old church is gone now, after my folks starved out so did our neighbors, and the church stood empty for years."

Another part of this book includes a letter a farmer wrote to relatives in 1937. He said, "I know you realize that the last 5 years have about ruined us financially. In 1934, we took a real spanking – had to part with 109 head of cattle on account of feed, and at those doggone prices! Have lost a lot of our good farmer friends. Most of them have gone to Minnesota to seek greener pastures. Lots of the land is going into the Federal Land Bank & Bank of North Dakota and so forth.

"You perhaps remember Pursian Lake. There is no lake anymore, and the buildings are half covered with sand. Of all the times Louis dived from the spring board Sunday afternoons! He used to steal the show. Some day soon, I expect to see the lake full of water.

"We wintered 65 cattle, 135 head of sheep, 8 horses, 75 hens, & 10 cats and we are getting by this year. Had a lot of snow and are thankful for that. The last 3 days have been warm and the snow is disappearing like fog. Last week, the 22nd, 23rd, & 24th we had a 3-day blizzard so bad it even hampered train service. Read in the papers airline service was the only transportation on schedule. No roads of any kind now, and I'm going to Bismarck tomorrow and might have to ride horseback to Steele.

"Tell the folks Hello and tell Louis to write and I will tell him about jack rabbits. Shorty was out one afternoon and shot 48 with his 22 rifle. Lately they flock together in big herds and have seen 75 more in one flock – never have seen anything like it before.

"Ducks we have none – have not shot one the last 4 years. Pheasants, yes. Had all we could eat last fall: had some hatch out in our turkey pasture."

The desperation of the people in these years is further portrayed in one of the author's chapters titled "The Exodus" (Vorthmann, *Church at Four Corners*, page 186), that recounts the struggles of those lean years. "They came in droves from northern Europe with hope in their souls. The thought of 160 acres of free land helped to overcome the fear of traveling across the ocean, leaving loved ones behind, and facing the unknown. Most of them stopped in the settled country of Wisconsin, Iowa, or Minnesota for a few years, generally living with relatives or friends until they could save enough to buy the supplies necessary to homestead. 160 acres of flat farm land sounded very good to the Norwegians where there is very little farm land. Little did they know that it was highly unlikely for them to be able to consistently earn a living on 160 acres in the Dakota prairie. They could not have imagined that there would be years with almost no rain and that crops planted would be more likely to blow away than to sprout. But come they did, picking carefully their homesteads, and putting up some crude shelter, as required, to more or less protect them from the elements.

"For some it was stay until they had met the requirements to obtain clear title to their land, then sell out, and move on. These perhaps were the lucky ones. For others, a few good wet years built confidence and they went into debt borrowing money from the willing banks, and used the money to build better houses, barns, buy more land, and to improve their herds etc. Then came the lean years, with very little rain and a wind that blew their soil away. There were cyclones that destroyed their precious buildings. Diseases like diphtheria and influenza took many lives, particularly children. Child bearing, which was often attended just by a midwife, was particularly difficult during these times. Sometimes it would result in the death of the mother, or the child would be stillborn or would have problems such as open spine, which could have been prevented with better diet. The number of children buried in Bethel Cemetery attests to the hardship of childbirth during these difficult times.

"Henry remembered the Depression in Baker Township as follows: 'From 1929 on thru the'30s every year became worse–no rain–crop failures every year–dry and hot summers. Pursian Lake dried up completely in 1933-34. Alkali dust from the bottom blew in the air constantly. It was like flour on the windows, sills, inside the house, where it crept through constantly. I tell you it was hard to bear. We had to sell cattle, horses, livestock, no hay to get. One year we cut Russian thistle for hay, kept it in the silo like silage. It was very bad for the cattle. Dad had gotten into debt with buildings he had built, no income of any kind, so it is no wonder so many had to leave their homes to seek a new future elsewhere. It was so very sad a time, everything seemed to change, it was a past era. The nice little farms and homesteads disappeared, one by one, only memories of the happy'20s remained. My folks had to leave in the fall of 1935 and moved to Park Rapids, Minnesota. They had to leave all they had built and struggled for. It was the hardest time of all to leave my boyhood home. I had been really happy there. The Pursian lake area had been such a thriving, happy neighborhood, a lovely church, nice country schools, a lively 4-H community. It had been really so great then.'

"The Depression caused some of them to commit suicide rather than face the reality of what life had dealt them. When they were unable to pay off their loans, the banks were all too eager to foreclose in order to get the title to the settlers' lands. Then there were sheriff's sales or if you were lucky you had your own sale, but the farm items you had for sale went very cheaply because nobody else had any money either. The tragic death of three of their friends and neighbors in a mysterious fire at Christmas time in 1934 cast a pall over the area. Then they left one by one until almost all of the Norwegians who had settled Baker township were gone. By now the banks were asking people to live free on the land which they had foreclosed on, but it was too late, the spirit of the community had been broken."

The author (Vorthmann, *Church at Four Corners*, page 187) continues, "The little church that had been built with so much pride and hope stood alone on the prairie surrounded by the grave markers of those who had passed on. As the settlers left the community there were fewer and fewer parishioners to support the church, and it was used only occasionally. As time moved on the church began to show the signs of neglect and by 1958 it was surrounded by weeds, and in need of paint. In 1962 some of the last members sold the building to a group from Moffit where it was used for services. With the church building gone the cemetery continued to decline. The families of local people who had relatives buried there, occasionally would mow the weeds on their family plot, but little by little even this declined. Those graves who did not have a local caretaker became hidden from view by the ever encroaching lilacs. Thus, what had been the hub of the spiritual and social life of a vibrant community became a weed-infested patch of ground surrounded by broken down fence with only a few headstones showing above the prairie."

After the experiences of this North Dakota cemetery restoration and the stories of these brave, courageous pioneers told in this remarkable book, *Church at Four Corners*, I have made it a practice to visit this cemetery every third year along with visits to two other cemeteries in Northern and Southern Minnesota where close relatives, with no other survivors, are buried. These cemeteries have quality perpetual care but this is no guarantee problems will not arise. Last year I found the large headstone for my father's and birth mother's graves in a cemetery in Minnesota was tilting about fifteen degrees. A letter to the man responsible for upkeep brought immediate repair but periodic surveillance by caring descendents is necessary.

When I am deceased, who will continue this effort? No one, I'm afraid. I've discussed this with some of my sons and daughters and they all profess some concern but I'm not confident this will translate into action. We're losing the concept of families in this country as an indispensable part of our life and this is tragic. Paying homage to our ancestors should be part of our obligations to their memory.

A tight knit family has been sacred for centuries. Try as we might to label it irrelevant, it remains the foundation for better relationships. It is the preferred way, the best way, for children to learn how to live their lives responsibly and wisely. Humans eventually adopt the characteristics of those with whom they associate daily. Live with troublemakers and become a troublemaker. Live with good people and you will become a good person. That's an axiom as old and as accurate as the history of man.

This is dependent, of course, on the character of the head of the family and other adults in the family but we are our associations, our relationships, whether it's family, school, church or anyone else with whom we spend our days and nights.

Are there lessons to be learned from the Great Depression days? Yes, there are. A stable loving family should be the objective to attain a better "house."

♦ Chapter Five: **WORK**

The average job in the 1930s meant long hours and low pay. Seventy-five dollars per month was typical for white color jobs, less for unskilled workers. Almost all jobs were five-and-one-half days which included a half a day on Saturday. Very few jobs required Sunday work as few stores or businesses were open on the Sabbath. In some neighborhoods all one could purchase on Sunday was a few items like milk and bread from a small convenience store.

There were significant differences between office and factory jobs in work rules and promotions but this comparison between the 1930s and today will be primarily with office and sales work. The big difference is how workers look at their jobs. In the 1930s jobs were a precious commodity. If you were lucky enough to have one, you did everything in your power to hold it. The unemployment rate was between thirty and forty percent. The unemployed were desperate for work but none was available.

It was especially difficult for young people who had neither experience nor a skill. The government began several programs during this time to provide some work. The most prominent was the CCCs or Civilian Conservation Corp (mentioned briefly in an earlier chapter). Young men who signed up were sent to various parts of the country to do work for the conservation of natural resources such as restoring parks, building shelters and campgrounds and clearing land and building roads in remote areas. They were given room, board and health care and were paid thirty dollars per month. Initial commitment was six months but men could reenroll for up to two years. Begun in 1933, over two and one-half million men in over one thousand camps passed through the CCC program by the time it was terminated in 1941. These programs helped immeasurably but unemployment remained high.

In addition, and for the first time in the history of the country, two large relief projects oriented to the general education of adults were begun. Men in the aforementioned CCCs were provided teachers and classes both in the camps and in adjacent educational facilities. At the same time a program was started to pay needy students in colleges ten to twenty dollars a month for part-time work customarily done by students working their way through school.

Concurrently with these relief programs, President Roosevelt demanded that those in charge of all these efforts keep politics out of them. A story in the *New York Times* on February 3, 1934, was headlined "President Demands Ban on Politics By Heads of Emergency Relief." It reported, "The President devoted the greatest part of his talk to condemning the evils of politics, selfish desires for personal credit in relief work and efforts to 'make political capital out of relief work.' These, he estimated, had caused 90 percent of the failures registered thus far. 'This work has nothing to do with partisan politics – nothing at all,' he explained. 'We are not the least bit interested in the partisan side of this picture.'"

Laudable words and goals but probably not much more successful than they would be today.

A considerable number of men "rode the rails" (hopped railroad freight cars) and moved from city to city living on handouts from the public. They were called bums or hobos but were not troublemakers, just men desperate for work. Those who had jobs protected them fiercely. Bosses were autocratic in their supervision because they knew, if you didn't like your job, they could get a hundred to replace you in a day.

Labor strikes were common and bitter in the 1930s. Workers without jobs were hungry. Companies usually prevailed in these disputes because there was simply no other work available. Many conflicts and resentments were born in those turbulent times that persisted for decades. Public sympathy for these disputes accelerated and then waned as economic conditions remained desperate and year-after-year of low employment continued.

Another outgrowth of those conditions was a rash of kidnappings. There were always a few people with substantial assets and they became targets for gangsters who kidnapped some member of the family and demanded a ransom for their safe return. One of the more famous kidnappings that gained national publicity was that of a St. Paul, Minnesota banker named Edward Bremer kidnapped from his car on a St. Paul street on January 17, 1934, for a $200,000 ransom. His father was owner of a large brewery in St. Paul and a personal friend of then President Franklin Roosevelt. This occurred after nine prominent kidnappings in the previous year, 1933. These were becoming so numerous that a national "hotline" number, NAtional 7117, was set up to report tips to federal authorities in Washington, D.C. Yes, that was the correct telephone number. You dialed NA (or 62) and then 7117. This hotline procedure was uncommon in the days when long distance calls were all handled manually by operators sitting in long rows in telephone buildings patching calls together on a "cord board" to make connections as the calls traveled across the country.

The ransom for Bremer was paid and he was shoved out of a car on a street in Rochester, Minnesota, about seventy-five miles south of St. Paul, after twenty-two days of captivity, dirty and disheveled and with a head laceration from his abduction, but otherwise unhurt. One man was ultimately apprehended for the kidnapping and sentenced to a long jail term but others were obviously involved. Many of these kidnapping gangs were captured, tried and convicted, but numerous kidnappings were never solved. They were indicative of the times, not unexpected given the conditions of those years.

On the farm, education often ended after the eighth grade but in the city most young people realized more education was important and tried to obtain a high school diploma if possible. College was rare for most high school graduates. The GI Bill of Rights, passed after World War II, paid college tuition for all returning veterans and that changed expectations for millions of young people. The GI Bill, technically known as the Servicemen's Readjustment Act, was passed by Congress in June, 1944. It provided several major benefits. Veterans were paid up to $500 per year for tuition and books (an adequate amount for those years) in colleges or training schools, and a subsistence allowance of $50 per month, later increased to $75 per month (again adequate for that time). Other provisions of the bill provided low cost loans to purchase a home or business, unemployment compensation of $20 per week for fifty-two weeks, if not in school (jokingly known as the 52-20 club), and, finally, assistance finding jobs.

Veterans enrolled en masse. Of sixteen million veterans, over two million enrolled in college under the GI Bill, three-and-one-half million in other schools and an additional two million in other training. That's about half of all veterans of World War II, an astounding percentage.

For the first time the majority of young people could attend college. This changed a generation, a society, and the country. The workforce was subsequently flooded with new engineers, lawyers, doctors, teachers and young people no longer satisfied to do menial tasks but wanting jobs where they could make use of their newly acquired brain power. Industry and commerce rushed to take advantage of all these educated people and soon computer designers and specialists, health care technicians, marketing executives and other professionals filled the ranks of workers and the information age was born, thanks in large part to the GI Bill.

As these GIs surged on to college campuses there was nominal friction between them and the regular students who were not happy with the crowded conditions that ensued. These students also had to work more diligently to keep up with the GIs who had just returned from a war and were eager to study long hours to make up lost time. The two factions learned to co-exist, however, and the atmosphere on campuses became more serious and businesslike with the GIs a major portion of the student body. In fact, in an article from the *Veterans of Foreign Wars* magazine in June/July 1994, by Lee Kennett, he reports, "University of Chicago President Robert Hutchins warned against admitting masses of veterans to institutions of higher education, saying the nation's campuses would become 'educational hobo jungles.' Quite the contrary occurred. Benjamin Fine, education editor for the *N.Y. Times*, wrote in Nov. 1947: '…Here is the most astonishing fact in the history of American higher education...The GIs are hogging the honor rolls and the Dean's lists; they are walking away with top marks in all of their courses...Far from being an educational problem, the veteran has become an asset to higher education.'"

Lee Kennett further claims in this same article, "Many who served in the war had been concerned that they were somehow marking time or even falling behind in realizing their hopes for home and family, rewarding careers, and 'the good life.' For these veterans, the GI Bill offered what sociologists call a 'bridging environment,' to a way of life that would have been unattainable otherwise."

The Great Depression of the 1930s that extended into World War II could have continued after the War when all those veterans were discharged in a short time period but the GI Bill prevented this from occurring. There are historians that say of all the bills ever passed by Congress this GI Bill may have been the most significant. That's a momentous statement, but consider these facts as outlined in an article in *The American Legion* magazine in August, 2001, by Michael J. Bennett. "GI Joe certainly could have gone on a monumental rampage in 1945-46. Civilian jobs had dropped from 63 million to 58 million as industry slowly converted to peacetime production. Coal, railroad and steel strikes were so massive President Harry Truman demanded power to conscript strikers, an unconstitutional interference with collective bargaining stopped by Sen. Robert Taft, R-Ohio, the Senate majority leader. Conflict raged, but the veterans, rather than being dragged in out of loyalty or necessity, stayed on the sidelines. Unemployment compensation tided over 9 million veterans; education enrolled 8.3 million, 2.2 million in college; no-down payment houses were bought by 6 million, and hundreds of thousands started businesses or professions, and unemployment rates remained about 3 percent."

But the GI Bill was not only an education bill. It triggered a housing boom, the birth of the suburbs and the movement of millions of families into middle class economic and social status.

Michael J. Bennett, in the aforementioned article, also gives the example of Levittown, the "nation's primordial suburb" where over seventeen thousand homes were built, priced at about $8,000, almost all for veterans with little down payment and a Veterans

Administration (GI Bill authorized) loan. He quotes a veteran's wife in this development saying, "It was only four rooms and a bath, but who cared? It was a beautiful thing. This was ours, our grass, our rooms, our everything."

Many of the GIs in this period were married or had plans to marry and needed housing immediately for a family. If they could not afford a "Levittown" home, it was common to see basement homes springing up all over the country. These were homes where the GI had just enough money to buy cement blocks and build the foundation themselves, cap it off, live in the basement until they had some more money to buy wood and continue with the walls, roof, interior and other parts of the house.

In other portions of the article Bennett argued that we should be exporting the concept and the framework of the GI Bill to third world countries as an example of how they could jumpstart their laggard economies. We might well have convinced Russia to adopt a plan similar to this bill after we had won the Cold War with them and they were trying to convert their economy, devoted solely to war material, to consumer goods. This may have made their shift from communism to a more democratic form of government less difficult.

What a model! If only some of our present day legislation could be half as successful. The example set by this GI Bill may be the best lesson the world could learn today for improving itself. Visualize what might happen if some of the poorest countries on this troubled globe were convinced and/or assisted to adopt their own "GI Bills" and educate their struggling, impoverished masses. Yes, many are run by despots, dictators, murderers and thugs, brutalizing their people, subjugating their women and plundering their resources, but that's another challenge. This might be a hundred times more effective than throwing billions of dollars of foreign aid money at these countries year after year which rarely reaches the people who desperately need it and is more frequently confiscated by their dictators for their years in opulent exile.

I doubt the GI bill is ever mentioned, much less explained, in any modern United States history textbook used in today's high schools and colleges. That's why we make the same mistakes over and over again. "Forget history," they say. "How can those white males teach us anything?"

As a final aside to this subject, you should know that the acronym "GI" stands for "government issue," hardly a great designation for a soldier on a battlefield risking life and limb, but apropos, I guess, to portray the soldier in that battle-scared war doing his duty for honor and country. "GI Joes" was also used interchangeably as a designation for these soldiers, sailors and marines.

The tools of the workplace were another major contrast in the two time periods. In the 1930s the major business tool was the manual typewriter. Copies were made with carbon paper while typing. There were crude adding machines, sometimes called "accounting machines" by salesmen, but they were slow and laborious to operate. Retail stores had cash registers that recorded the amount of each sale and a total for the day but little more.

World War II accelerated quick printing and calculating devices, however. Several systems were introduced where masters or mats or forms could be prepared on a typewriter and then attached to a drum or roller in a duplicating machine to produce multiple copies for the office or factory. Some of these were messy and cumbersome compared to today's copying systems but a real leap forward from the typewriter and carbon paper. These marvels of the business world, as they were touted in advertisements, were accompanied by more sophisticated adding and calculating machines that could perform operations heretofore impossible but now desperately needed to produce material and products for the war effort. During this time, and in the 1940s, eighty-column punched card tabulating machines also came into use.

In the retail field no modern department store or bank was without a pneumatic tube system using air pressure to push some type of carrier holding money or documents. They remain in use today most visibly in bank drive-up operations, but also in hospitals and other areas where it is essential to transfer the original documents back and forth instead of data in a computer network. What made them unique in the 1930s was they were usually visible to the customer, out in the open, so to speak.

I remember as a child of seven or eight years I would go with my stepmother to a clothing store where the clerk would write up a sales slip for whatever we purchased, take our money, and stuff all of it into a cylindrically shaped tube and send the tube along some rails or tracks high up in the ceiling of the store to a central location. I would wait expectantly and, sure enough, in a minute or two that tube would come rattling back with our change in it. I always wondered who or what was pushing it and would we see our change again or would it maybe disappear in that noisy, clanging equipment. Today's systems are usually quiet by comparison, invisible en route and probably computer controlled. It didn't take much for us to be mesmerized in those days, a marked contrast to the children of today.

In the industrial field engineers relied on slide rules, not computers. For those who haven't seen a slide rule it's about a one-foot-long rule with a sliding piece marked in a logarithmic scale, moveable against a stationery part also marked logarithmically, offering rapid calculation of large numbers. Also, the concept of the "assembly line" where products move down a line as they are being built, and workers stationed all along the line perform repetitive tasks on each unit as it passes them, had been well established in previous decades and was essential to the mass production needed in the war effort.

If you lived on a farm, even manual typewriters and carbon paper were foreign objects. The dust bowl travails of farmers in the Midwest, who had the choice of immigrating west or starving to death, have been well documented in books and movies of that period. Lesser known are the thousands of farmers who remained on their land and eked out a bare subsistence for several years in the 1930s. Power was supplied by horses. Tractors were rare and too expensive to own. Physical labor, of everyone in the family over five-years of age, was required and many families survived on what they could grow in a garden. One year dust storms would wipe out whatever crop came up, the next year there would be no crop at all because there was zero rain, and then the following year hordes of grasshoppers or some other insect would descend on the few blades of grain foolish enough to rise above the ground. This catastrophe was covered in a previous chapter but it bears repeating here because it was a terrible period for agriculture and many eighty-year-olds today remain molded and warped by the memory of those horrible years.

Farmers who had prospered in earlier years were wiped out in the 1930s. Farm auction sales were a weekly event and farmers sold every item on the farm or in the house to get a few dollars, sometimes pennies, to exist for a while and move on. Summers were difficult but winters were equally tough. One family told me they had so much snow they shoveled tunnels *under the snow* to reach the barn, the well or other buildings. Nature was cruel in summer and winter. There was no let up: blazing heat in the summer, mind-numbing cold in the winter.

Farmers forced off their farms frequently just left without a trace and title to the land eventually reverted to the local bank. These banks were land rich but profit poor because they could not find anyone to work the land under any arrangements, on shares, cash rent or other terms. Why work someone else's land (the bank's) when your crop was wiped out each year? Half of nothing was still nothing!

I've talked to friends who went through the Great Depression on those farms and they will never, ever forget those years. Discuss with them today's farming methods where a farmer climbs into an air-conditioned tractor or threshing machine cab, checks his computer for fertilizing or seeding percentages and turns on his stereo to hear soft music – or maybe heavy metal – and they can't come to grips with what you're outlining to them. They remember farming as an isolated, dismal, backbreaking life of hard labor and no amount of twenty-first century technology will ever alter that viewpoint. Rational? Maybe not. But that's their memory of those years and nothing will change that as long as they live.

That life is epitomized for me by a life-size statue that stands today outside a local company in the neighborhood where I live. The statue, about six feet tall, is a farmer in old-fashioned bib overalls, work shirt rolled up to the elbows, broad brimmed hat (obviously before baseball caps), and heavy booted shoes. He is bent slightly at the waist, tying the top of a large gunnysack, probably with some type of grain in it. Each time I look at this statue I see more meaning in it.

My first look was several years ago and all I saw was a farmer busy at work. As I observed it on subsequent occasions I began to see hard labor on his part, then old-fashioned value in his plain dress, then honesty and simplicity in the work he is doing which is needed to feed people and, finally, admiration for the bygone values of unpretentious work done conscientiously.

It's easy to visualize this farmer returning home in the evening to a square, two-story, simple wood farmhouse. The first floor would have a bedroom and living room on one side with a large kitchen and open porch on the other side. The second story would be three bedrooms, one above each of the downstairs rooms, a practical design for the large families of early homesteads. Add a barn, an outhouse and other assorted outbuildings and that's a picture repeated tens of thousands of times in early Midwest rural communities.

Do we have any of the values today suggested by that statue in my neighborhood? Very few, I venture. We can use super computers at our desks and perform miracles this simple farmer never dreamed of, but are we proud of what we do and strive to do it better or are we just marking time?

Notwithstanding doubts about attitude, the technology of today's computing industry, and associated industries, make it a clear winner over the technology of any other period in history and the major reason for myriad advancements in our present society. This fact stands alone as a major achievement of today's world.

At this juncture I must take liberty with the definition of work, which is the focus of this chapter, and broaden my next recollections to cover an advancement in technology in today's world that has probably been superseded only by nuclear energy and medical science. That's the technology of telecommunications. Once a stodgy science with one company holding a pure monopoly, modern telecommunications have made possible the Internet, cell phones, long distance calls for pennies per minute and remote systems for performing almost any task known to man or woman, in the office, in the factory or on the road.

This saga commenced with the Communications Act of 1934 passed by Congress with the goal of universal telephone service and establishment of the Federal Communications Commission (FCC) to regulate the interstate portions of it. The "Bell System," as it was usually known, consisted of The American Telephone and Telegraph Company (better known as AT&T), its seven regional operating companies (the "Baby Bells" as they were called with some derision), the equipment supplier, Western Electric Co., and the long distance business controlled by AT&T as the "holding company" for all of the above. This consortium plodded along through the next several decades with only modest advancements in technology.

In the 1930s, if you lived in the city, telephones were all black, rotary dial phones. The numbers were all a combination of two letters and four digits, for example, LOcust 1234, REgent 1234 or WAlnut 1234. There were no area codes. A long distance call was made by dialing the telephone operator in your city or town and she (it was always a woman) would patch your call through manually to its destination.

If you lived in the country, you probably had a system that required calling the local operator for all calls or maybe cranking a lever on the phone box to signal your intentions. In the simplest of systems, each farm might have a different number of cranks or rings as their "number." Two turns of the crank might be the farm one mile south of your farm, three cranks the farm two miles east, etc. It might have been rudimentary but it worked, after a fashion, at least, although the loud cranks which were heard up and down the system alerted everyone who wanted to eavesdrop to hurry to their phone.

The next most prominent communications capability for residential users was telegrams handled by just one company, Western Union Telegraph Co. Telegrams were relatively expensive but provided proof of delivery and a hard copy the recipient could hold in their hand and refer to. However, the arrival of a Western Union messenger on his bicycle usually meant bad news. Telegrams were transmitted between Western Union offices all over the country on their private lines by telegraph machines with paper tape output. This tape was cut and pasted on a telegram form to convey a message like "Uncle Bob died yesterday STOP funeral Thursday at ten o'clock STOP hope you can be there." STOP was used in lieu of punctuation. It made a rather messy telegram if the message was long but served its purpose. During World War II no family with a member in service wanted to see a Western Union messenger approaching the house as that was the method the government used to notify families of servicemen or women killed or missing in action.

After World War II cracks occurred in the AT&T monopoly, however, as technology advanced outside the Bell System, and clamored for a piece of the business. On January 1, 1984, after long, contentious legal proceedings, the monopoly was broken up (it was called "divestiture") and progress of immense proportions began.

The Internet we have today, an evolution of extraordinary proportions, would never be possible without divestiture. One company could not have invented and produced the equipment and operating systems required for this phenomenal advancement in modern history. Hundreds, probably thousands of companies have been contributors to it. Originally conceived in academia, the Internet has become a reality only with the recent technological advancements in telecommunications. But these advancements in telecommunications go deeper than just the Internet. It's local service (the line into each residence or business), and all the bells and whistles on your home phone, a staggering array of new products, and long distance and remote capabilities unheard of just a decade ago.

There are people in telecommunications, both users and suppliers, who foolishly wish for the old system with one bill to pay and one company to blame. Fortunately, they are not listened to. Prices for new products and the cost of long distance calls have plummeted. Who could have envisioned a decade or two ago buying a telephone for fifty dollars versus having to rent it for ten dollars a month FOREVER, or making a long distance call from coast to coast for five cents a minute or less versus fifty cents or a dollar a minute not so many years ago?

The only problem in this brilliant new technology remains local service. Local service is that service you receive from the company who has installed the line into your home or business and furnished the dial tone you get when you pick up the phone to make a call. It is alleged by most of the competitors of these companies that they maintain a stranglehold on their territories through the facilities they have in place to provide local service to all their subscribers. This stranglehold is also buttressed, according to competitors, by the facilities the local service companies own to connect incoming and outgoing long distance calls to telephones outside their territories. It is alleged that these services (called interconnection), are charged to them at higher prices than are warranted by their cost. Every government agency from the fifty states to the FCC and Congress has tried to solve this problem but to no avail. The companies with the existing franchises, all of which are regulated to some degree, and operate under the sanction (or at least the blessing) of some government agency, maintain they must receive higher revenues for these services and any encroachment on their present rates would put them out of business.

It's a long boring story, but regulators, historically sympathetic to residential telephone users, and unable to determine the actual cost of these services, have authorized telephone companies to charge higher rates to business customers to subsidize residential service at lower rates. Various other subsidy schemes, not apparent to the user, to cover all manner of social tinkering, are also buried in the rate everyone pays for basic telephone service. Consequently, the cost structure of the entire industry is out of whack and existing companies providing local service, in an amazing charade of deception and obfuscation, say rates have no where to go but up, not down and the song and dance of who should pay for what goes on endlessly.

As a result, telephone cost accounting systems, since the invention of sending a message on a string between two tin cans, has been a black hole of deceit and duplicity augmented by industry and government subsidies and controlled by parties interested only in maintaining the status quo. This dilemma in local service will not be solved until wireless technology advances to the point where competitors can offer duplicate facilities ("overbuild" as it's termed in the industry), and established companies are forced to meet this competition for the first time in their corporate lives. Wireless technology (no physical lines into a house or telephone poles in the street) is not quite there yet but it is closing in fast on whole-service capability.

Today consumers with cell phones often roam around their house using their cell phone in place of the hard-wired phone they've had for years. So why not disconnect that old phone, get some more cell phone handsets, and use those exclusively? Some practical reasons remain why this is not the best answer at this time. It's not quite cost effective yet, coverage is spotty in some areas, and extensions will probably require a base station device to operate efficiently and conveniently. Security can also be a problem. Unlike systems connected by wires, a lone motorist, with intercept devices (called hackers in the corporate world), in a residential neighborhood of wireless systems, could tap into any system lacking security provisions. Corporations, hospitals and educational institutions, however, are installing wireless local area networks (called WLANs) in large numbers and some of these corporate systems have thousands of stations or extensions on their network serving multiple applications. The technology is there. It just requires some tweaking to serve residential customers. But that's the future, almost here, but not quite. This is Buck Rogers stuff, by the way, for folks from the 1930s.

When that completely wireless day arrives, the local telephone company will be forced to lower their rates or go out of business. The basic rate for residential telephone service will plunge to five to ten dollars a month (plus taxes) from the current twenty-five dollars per month. This will be similar to decreases in long distance rates we have already experienced from fifty cents per minute to five cents per minute or less and the huge reductions in telephone equipment prices that enable us to buy telephone products from multiple sources versus having to rent them each month from the local telephone company.

A final note on the labyrinthine byways of telecommunications is an explanation of the line item on all your local service and long distance telephone bills labeled "Federal tax." Believe it or not that's a three percent excise tax created in 1898 (that's right 1898) to help pay for the Spanish-American War. In the intervening years its been increased and decreased several times, and multiple efforts made to kill it, but over one hundred years later anyone with a telephone continuous to pay that tax. Who said only death and taxes are equal certainties in this world? Death comes sooner for most of us!

Much like the treatise on grasshoppers in Chapter One this is probably more than you want to know about telecommunications but it's so significant today, in our work and in our play, it compels this explanation. Besides the Internet, besides hand-held computer-phones, besides talking frequently on the phone to your son or daughter away in college for pennies a day, consider the safety protection of remote phones for women, teens, accident victims and many other uses we now take for granted. These are all a part of this new, revolutionary technology known as telecommunications.

Has the Internet, made possible by these advances, been an unblemished success? Of course not. Few advancements in our lives are. It's undoubtedly facilitated the dissemination of pornography, a scourge to society that threatens to envelope all of us, advanced the art of cheating in schools by students discovering sources to buy information rather than digging it out from libraries and gluing some of us to a system of chat rooms and nonsensical, ungrammatical e-mail that lowers human intelligence rather than raising it.

Skeptics have even said in referring to the Internet, "We invented a catastrophe!" That's probably hyperbole but there is usually a price to pay for every advancement and the Internet via the wonders of telecommunications is no exception.

But this history of telecommunications has been inserted for another reason, Significant as it is, it's an example of a technological advancement that has brought untold benefits to society but has not yet reached its potential. Its recent history has been rife with squabbling from industry and regulators alike about who will be allowed to do what. During this political malaise innovation suffers. The lesson? Technology alone is not enough!

Obviously, there is more to civilization. Humans are identified by morals, standards, relationships, responsibilities and compassion for each other (or the lack thereof) and these hallmarks of a society have little connection to technology. In the 1930s workers received a certain satisfaction, a degree of pride, in turning out a clean report on a typewriter or a fine looking chair in a factory. They were close to the product, they knew their skill and their commitment made a difference in the quality of that product. I doubt today's workers feel a similar satisfaction. Workers on a factory assembly line may perform one thousand repetitive motions a day as a small part of a product they never see after it is completed. In the office most workers sitting at a computer terminal haven't the foggiest notion of how or why that terminal is working but, lo and behold, if they punch the right keys each time, it spits out something someone uses somewhere so why question what they are doing? We hear the phrase everywhere we go, "The computer's down. I can't help you." What does "down" mean? They haven't the slightest idea.

For the average worker we've changed from a personal workplace where they could have satisfaction in their performance to an impersonal, repetitive routine susceptible to carpal tunnel syndrome and other stress related enigmas.

This attitude manifests itself in the lack of loyalty today's workers have to their company and the company to the worker. Several friends my age have retired from companies where they worked forty to fifty years. It was their only job. They stayed with that company through good times and bad. They truly felt a loyalty to that employer. Companies reciprocated. In bad times layoffs were the last action taken. Now they're the first action.

Interestingly, one company was publicized recently for employing only older workers, mostly over seventy years of age, and some in their nineties. The company said older workers were more dependable and careful – but also resistant to change. Workers said never retiring kept them alert and healthy and with goals to achieve, vital at any age.

The 1940s and the World War II years brought profound change, however. Men went off to military service and women stepped in to fill the void. Their contributions were incalculable. Women learned welding, carpentry and many other skills including becoming pilots ferrying aircraft to all parts of the world. The war could not have been won without their contributions. Posters acclaimed their exploits and the image of "Rosie the Riveter," as they were appropriately named, inspired women to heights they had never achieved previously. These war years were filled with posters everywhere urging the public to "Buy Bonds" or reminding them that "Loose Lips Sink Ships" but the most memorable for me was the poster of "Rosie" with her arm doubled back to show a bulging muscle and the headline "We Can Do It!" This was revolutionary in an era where women had just escaped the notion they were incapable of performing any task other than typing, nursing or teaching school.

Today it's taken for granted that women can perform all the jobs men can do but it took a World War in the 1940s to demonstrate this. Chalk up another huge advantage for that period as a harbinger for subsequent events in the workplace.

Our attitudes toward work today are casual: Everyone is owed a job and easy does it! Once again this attitude comes from no appreciation for history. The prevailing thought among elites is that this country has learned to control the business cycle and we will never have another depression. That's nonsense but understandable given the teaching today in our schools that ignores the lessons of history. We have always had wars and always will have wars. Economic cycles – recessions, depressions, boom times – will repeat themselves. The fortunes of man and country ebb and flow throughout time and always will.

Consequently, workers can't visualize a time when they may be unemployed for years and would give anything in their power for a job, any job. This feeling of job entitlement is stronger the younger the person. I would guess some of my sons and daughters share it. I know the majority of my grandchildren believe they will always be able to leave a job and walk into another one the following week with no difficulty. If you examine history, even casually, you'll see how foolish that is. Now, when the economy is stronger, is the time to learn to hold on to a job, respect the rewards it gives you, and prepare for better ones.

I will never forget the example of a teacher in a one-room schoolhouse in Iowa in 1934 where I was a pupil for a short period of time. My stepmother remarried and we moved to her new husband's farm in northern Iowa. At the age of ten I walked two miles to school along a dusty gravel road barely wide enough for two cars to pass. Early morning was a magical time in the country. Birds flitted about singing their siren songs and filling their stomachs with plump seeds available everywhere. Cows in our pasture looked at me anew each morning with a blank, quizzical stare as if I had just arrived from another planet. The school had five pupils, one in the first grade, one in the third, one in the fourth and one in the eighth grade. I was in the fifth grade. I only attended this school for six months as my stepmother's husband died suddenly and we moved back to Minneapolis but I remember the dedication of this teacher. Each pupil had four subjects and she spent a few minutes with each of us on every subject every day. That's twenty subjects to teach!

In addition, she tended the wood stove, cleaned the outhouse, washed the windows, did some painting and even repaired textbooks so they wouldn't fall apart during the school year. All this was performed with cheerfulness and optimism for our future, especially on our birthdays when we would all make homemade cards to give the birthday celebrant. This teacher had never heard about long hours, poor pay, class size or "teaching to rule." She did her best with whatever she had to work with and never grumbled about anything that I can recall. This was a person skilled in her work, dedicated to her work and, as I recollect at that early age, enjoyed her work.

How different today. When one called a company in the 1930s (yes, we did have telephones) to order a product or service, a human being always answered. A call today is apt to bring a recorded message and a long litany of choices, all prefaced with "press one" or "press two," or whatever, and sending you on more branch routes than an octopus. Eventually one may hear a live voice but just as frequently get, "Leave your name, street address, city, state, zip code, telephone number, with area code, date of birth, social security number, and the reason for your call. Begin talking at the sound of the tone and speak slowly and distinctly. We'll return your call as soon as possible. Thank you and have a good day." Ugh!

Also lost in the nuances and deferments of this type of "service" is a deliberate purpose to avoid personal contact with the customer or complainant at all costs. Life has been too easy in recent years. People have lots of money, products fly off the shelf, services can be avoided or delayed with little penalty and customer satisfaction is an ephemeral concept easily replaced by new sales and new customers. The customer is no longer a real voice, a live body. He or she is a statistic. How old are they, how much did they spend, and how did they pay, supercedes that old-fashioned term, "The customer is always right."

Companies and corporations are responsible for this attitude under the guise of reducing costs. It's especially onerous if one is trapped between two companies or two service agencies (like government and/or the health care industry) where one can blame the other. The customer is a Ping-Pong ball between despair and futility. These lackadaisical attitudes today are a major, major difference from the 1930s.

Are there lessons to be learned from the Great Depression days? Yes, there are. In work, technology is a clear winner at the beginning of the twenty-first century, but wouldn't it be more satisfying if we felt better about what we do, try to improve how we do it and give the customer a feeling of importance again? And maybe study the GI Bill for guidance in assisting other countries?

◆Chapter Six: **MUSIC**

Superiority in music is heavily in favor of the 1930s.

Young people today, when reminded of the "oldies," as they call them, believe there was only slow, sweet music. That was part of it, and a glorious part, but the early 1930s to the mid-1940s was also the heyday of jazz and jazz tempos can be fast or slow. One characteristic that distinguishes 1930s music from today is comprehensible lyrics. Each syllable of a vocal was clear and understandable.

The 1930s was also the heyday of the big bands. These were bands with twenty, thirty, often more, musicians. Paradoxically, it was easier to support large bands in the depression era because each player received a small salary, and public support was outstanding for popular bands. Their demise, unfortunately, began in World War II when many players entered military service and traveling conditions deteriorated. Bands of that size playing popular music have never been as numerous since that period. Their size is one reason they were so musically outstanding. As the war progressed trios and quintets became popular and prevailed for many years.

In the 1930s young people my age were just as entranced by this music as young people are entranced with theirs today. Few of us could afford to purchase records but we listened to them on jukeboxes at every opportunity. Jukeboxes were everywhere, in hamburger joints, restaurants, pool halls, bars, clubs, ballrooms, dance halls and youth centers. Records were all 78s (or 78rpm), which remained popular until after World War II, although 33s and 45s became popular long before the demise of 78s. The original 78s were made of some kind of material containing copious amounts of shellac. They were easily scratched and broken and required care in handling. These were replaced by vinyl in the 1930s, as I remember, and "platters" have been all vinyl since that time. Aficionados of these things claim vinyl records have a superior sound to compact disks (CDs), and I wouldn't argue with that, but CDs have a big advantage in handling and convenience. Like all else, however, tastes and tides are cyclical and many young people today are discovering their grandparent's old collections of vinyl records in the attic or in other storage and, after dusting them off and playing them, reveling in the "new" sound.

Most restaurants had a remote selection device in every booth so a patron could make selections while eating and keep the centrally located jukebox playing without leaving the booth. The cost for one play? FIVE CENTS! It was fascinating to sit in a booth, make a selection, and watch the arm on the huge Wurlitzer (which most of them were) jukebox move out in search of the record one had just chosen, retrieve it, plunk it down on the turntable and begin playing, a kaleidoscope of sight and sound, with all the lights flashing on and off in the "big box" as this process unfolded.

Does it sound like we were easily satisfied in those days? Yes, I suppose it does but we didn't have much so visualize it in that context.

In the evening radio programming was filled with dance bands, another name for big bands. After the nightly news, only fifteen minutes from ten o'clock to ten fifteen, there was dance music on several stations, occasionally from local hotels or ballrooms, but mostly from night spots on the East Coast or Chicago. We could get Glen Miller, Tommy Dorsey, Harry James or a similar band every night until late in the evening. Other popular bands were Louie Armstrong, Lionel Hampton, Count Basie, Artie Shaw, Billy Eckstine, the Dorsey Brothers, Jimmy and Tommy, Earl Hines, Fletcher Henderson, Glen Gray, Charlie Barnett, Cab Calloway, Erskine Hawkins, Claude Thornhill, Woody Herman, Vaughn Monroe and Gene Krupa to name just a few.

In the late 1930s small combos, three or four players, became popular. There were too many to mention but outstanding in my mind is the Nat 'King' Cole trio. Few people remember that Nat Cole was one of the greatest jazz pianists of all time before he became an outstanding success as a vocalist.

All these bands had male or female vocalists, often both, and after success with a big band, many embarked on a solo career. The most famous is probably Frank Sinatra, who began singing in 1940 with the Harry James band, then Tommy Dorsey, but soon began a permanent solo career. In my opinion the greatest female jazz singer of all time was Billie Holiday. Born in 1915 she died prematurely in 1959. She was a jazz singer but excelled at slow tempos, so slow, in fact, you were mesmerized by her beat wondering if she would sing another word after the one she was holding. She had a horrific life marked by poverty, alcohol, drugs, sex and, most of all, crushing racism. Two disastrous marriages (possibly three, even that's in doubt) added to her problems and framed a torturous but incredibly talented life.

Discovered in the mid-thirties she sang briefly in 1938 and 1939 with the bands of Count Basie and Artie Shaw but, thereafter, began a solo career. Her idol was Louis Armstrong and his singing and his trumpet. Her voice, before it disintegrated in drugs, alcohol and cigarettes, was unlike any other singer. During World War II she was the queen of West Fifty-second Street in Manhattan in jazz joints named Jimmy Ryan's, Kelly's Stables and the Famous Door. Fifty-second Street was jazz street in those years and patrons lucky enough to hear her at that time saw and heard her at her peak. Even then, however, drugs and alcohol were beginning to take a toll and her reputation for unreliability and irrationality was increasing.

If the song allowed, she sang slowly and seemed to go slower as the song progressed. But you didn't mind. You just wanted her to keep singing, to never finish. She sang the tragedy she lived and you could visualize that as you listened to her. Beyond this, she was a strong woman. If that seems contradictory, it was, but it was necessary for her to survive her life style. Racism played a large part in her misfortunes. Her stint with Artie Shaw and his all-white band would have been longer and eminently successful if hotels where they played, even in the North, had not barred her from using their facilities. One hotel even barred her from appearing with the band on the bandstand. A white female singer had to be available to substitute on the songs arranged solely for Billie Holiday's style. All black bands were allowed and, of course, all white but not mixed races. That was 1939 in the entertainment industry. It was a segregated world.

That same year she began singing a song named *Strange Fruit*, with a strong anti-lynching message, that portrayed the aftermath of a lynching in the South. It became one of her most requested numbers in New York nightclubs and for several years she always closed her sets with that song. Prominent recording houses would not record *Strange Fruit* because of opposition to the lyrics from their Southern dealers but eventually it was recorded and remains one of Billie Holiday's trademarks. Only two other artists have recorded this song.

One of my major regrets is never seeing Billie Holiday perform in person. But some of her most ardent fans today are people like me who never had the opportunity to listen to her live but Billie's incredible talent and the pathos in her performances live on for us in her recordings and the numerous biographies written about her. Ironically, her finest singing, in my opinion, was never on an album but was recorded in the soundtrack of a movie named *New Orleans* where she sang, *Do You Know What it Means to Miss New Orleans*, *Endie* and *The Blues are Brewin'* with feeling and clarity and the essence of tragedy no other singer has ever equaled.

New Orleans was a movie made in 1947, and noteworthy for its omission of racial stereotypes. A brief early sequence portrayed Billie Holiday as a maid and gave activists an opportunity to criticize the movie as demeaning to blacks but it overwhelmingly showcased the talents of Holiday and Louis Armstrong. It also told the story of the emerging popularity of jazz and black musicians in New Orleans in the 1917 to 1920 era after World War I. Jazz lovers differ on the birthplace of jazz but it certainly came to prominence in those years in the old Storyville section of New Orleans. The movie tells that story and the subsequent closing of Storyville at the behest of the military for perceived degradation in the area. After that closing the mostly black musicians scattered to other cities and thus spread the emerging allure of jazz to the entire country. There is a tender love story in this movie by two talented actors, Dorothy Patrick and Arturo De

Cordova, but it's the singing of Billie Holiday and the music of Louis Armstrong that make this a "must see" movie for jazz lovers.

In his decades of leading bands Armstrong had many talented musicians and an all-star cast was assembled for the nine musical numbers in the movie *New Orleans*. Barney Bigard is on clarinet, Zutty Singleton on drums, Kid Ory on slide trombone, Red Callendar on bass, Bud Scott on guitar and Charley Beal on piano.

But the star of the show is Holiday. If this sounds unlikely in view of the troubles she experienced in the World War II years, it is not, She was only thirty-two years of age when this movie was made and her irrational habits may have been escalating but her magical voice was never more pure, more vibrant, more poignant. *New Orleans* was Billie Holiday once again at her peak, the very essence of her career. If you can get this movie, you will play it over and over. She gets better each time you listen to it.

Every Holiday fan has their favorite songs but mine, along with the ones from the movie *New Orleans*, are those she sang at the end of her career when her voice was gone but her feelings vibrated in every note. Her recordings from the Monterey Jazz Festival of 1958, *When Your Lover Has Gone, Good Morning Heartache* and *Trav'lin Light* are unforgettable. I listen to them when I'm sad or melancholy and need to realize these kinds of emotions are universal.

Tributes by the thousands have been paid to Holiday but none more befitting than those in an insert to a compact disk titled *Billie Holiday Greatest Hits*, released in 1998 by Sony Music Entertainment Inc./Manufactured by Columbia Records/550 Madison Ave., New York, NY, and attributed to Timme Rosenkrantz and Inez Cavanaugh in the original LP liner notes: "She sang like an instrument, a whole orchestra. Sometimes there was the soft wail of a saxophone, then the piercing, sharply defined blast of a trumpet. Her voice crept under her skin and stayed there. I've never heard anyone else sing like Billie. Her phrasing was a heart-to-heart conversation with the world out there, so personal it gave one the feeling of being taken into strictest confidence by someone who had such a desperate need to 'tell it all,' that it seemed somehow sacred. This was the whole meaning of jazz – how it should be sung and never was, until Billie sang it."

Billie Holiday died in July, 1959, in a city hospital in Harlem, alone and penniless except for a few dollars taped to her leg. Writers have said some of her songs were really prayers. I hope hers were answered.

There were other great vocalists of this era such as Sarah Vaughan, Dinah Washington, Billy Eckstine, Carmen McRae, Julie London in the 1940s, and, yes, Louis Armstrong, remembered more for his band and his trumpet but a singer who expressed, incredibly, the feeling of what he was singing. These just happen to be my favorites, which I hope some readers share, but not meant to be a complete list in any respect.

Living in Minnesota we were not on the beaten path of big bands or jazz artists but occasionally some strayed north from Chicago and appeared in Minneapolis or St. Paul. Unlike today, small clubs and jazz joints were numerous in the 1930s featuring vocalists, trios and jazz artists. One of my favorites was a small band led by the legendary trumpet player Henry"Red" Allen and featuring for many years his lifelong friend, the incomparable J.C. Higginbothom on trombone. Allen also favored a drummer named Alvin Burroughs and I was fortunate enough to see them in live appearances in Minneapolis and in New York.

In Minneapolis they played the small clubs downtown. Between sets they would walk out to the sidewalk to smoke and this was a wonderful opportunity to walk outside with them and say a few words. Musicians in these years were gracious beyond belief and it was a joy to ask them where they were going next or maybe request a special number. Later, in the 1950s, I was fortunate to hear Allen again on several occasions when he had a long engagement at New York's Metropole on Broadway in Times Square. A small club, the doors usually open in the summer, you could hear his trumpet several doors away as you neared the club.

Playing with big bands early in his career, he was the leader of small jazz groups the last half of his career until his death in 1967. Few remember that Henry "Red" Allen, born in 1908, was often touted as another Louis Armstrong. He was a talented singer and featured vocalist on many of his recordings. Fame equaling Louis Armstrong never materialized but Allen was a jewel in the jazz world, probably under-appreciated as such, when we look back today at those heady jazz years of the 1930s and 1940s.

So my favorite vocalists are Billie Holiday, first, Sarah Vaughan, second, and Nat "King" Cole, third. Regrettably I never saw either of the three in person but they are alive for me in my collection of records, cassettes and CDs.

Sarah Vaughan could have been an opera singer. Her voice had over a three-octave range. Billy Eckstine, her lifelong friend, said it was another instrument. Born in 1924 she improved with age, was at her peak just before she died in 1990 at the age of sixty-six. If she sang in a big hall or arena, her voice would resonate throughout the area. She'd take over the audience, even the musicians-in-waiting, who would listen to her like amateurs. In a small club she was incomparable.

Sarah also frequently suffered race discrimination. The most egregious example of this was the type of songs she was given to record by her recording companies for much of her career. They were mostly second-rate songs, particularly the first half of her career, and this prevented her from enjoying the fame that less talented white singers experienced.

But she was never a pushover in her private life. Known as "Sassy" to her friends, or just "Sass," she was married and divorced four times, most of these husbands her managers. Billy Eckstine called them "damagers" but always listened sympathetically to Sarah when she complained to him. A very joyful personality to her fans and the masters of ceremony who introduced her, she was, to all, simply "The Divine One."

My favorite recordings of Sarah Vaughan are so numerous they must be segmented. In her early days she sang such simple standards as *Body and Soul* and *Somewhere Over the Rainbow* like no other singer has ever sung them. My favorite jazz recording is *Lullaby of Birdland*. She sang duets so well with Billy Eckstine, their recording of *I've Got my Love to Keep me Warm* is without equal. Of course, they sang it *We've Got our Love to Keep us Warm*.

Her finest ballad is *Send in the Clowns*. *Clowns* is not one of my favorite songs but Sarah Vaughan elevated it to a level beyond unbelievable. It is surely one of her most superb works. Two others (and there are so many) are *September Song* and *April in Paris* recorded first in 1954 on the original LP entitled simply *Sarah Vaughan* and released in 1990 on a CD by *Verve* with the same title.

These aren't just superb. They reach heights maybe no other female vocalist has ever reached in the popular genre.

There were other stars in this period. Perhaps the sweetest of the sweet bands was Tommy Tucker whose signature was "Tommy Tucker Time." In a career that peaked in the 1930s and early 1940s he played all the popular hotels and ballrooms on the East Coast and was on eight or ten popular radio programs either as a backup band or as his own show. His band had innumerable national recordings and hit tunes, but *I Couldn't Sleep a Wink Last Night*, with vocals by the group called "The Three Two-Timers," epitomized his style and seduction for a depression era audience looking for romance, i.e., a "sweet time."

A female vocalist, who had a long and exceptional career, and probably under-appreciated, was Peggy Lee. Duke Ellington said she was "beyond category," his highest praise for a performer. Born in 1920, she had an illustrious legacy of hit recordings before she died in 2002 at the age of eighty-one. As both a product of the 1930s and a contemporary, that longevity probably allowed people to take her for granted. Her jazz was slow but the kind that mesmerized as she sang tunes like *Why Don't You Do Right, Fever, Is That all There Is* and *I Love Being Here with You.*

I was fortunate to see her in person near the end of her career at a hotel in downtown Minneapolis where her faithful fans lined up for a memorable evening of the incomparable Peggy Lee, a phrase thrown around at abandon by many, but on target to describe her. She grew on me. The first time I heard her I said, "She's pretty good." The fourth or fifth time I said, "She's sensational, the way she sings her songs: plaintive, husky, almost reluctantly, with a melancholy lilt I've never heard before." That was Peggy Lee: fascinating and beautiful!

The list of my favorite singers, and I hope the favorites of many old-time music lovers, would not be complete without mentioning Una Mae Carlisle. Born in 1915, and labeled by some, mistakenly, I believe, as a second-rate singer, she had an up-and-down career. She was an excellent pianist and composer of many of her songs. This was another singer who was hurt by the recording ban during the World War II years. For parts of 1942 and 1943 (thirteen-and-one-half months) singers could record, instrumentalists could not, so singers recording with vocal groups as backup were common but not very successful.

Una Mae had a low, husky, throaty voice that riveted one to her lyrics. She began her career at the age of sixteen in 1931 under the tutelage of Fats Waller with whom she remained friends until his early death in 1943. Her songs had a reputation for being danceable, both fast and slow, but illness struck during the World War II years and her last records were cut in 1950. She died in New York in 1956. I have three CDs of her music, all issued recently, and labeled Una Mae Carlisle 1938-1941, Una Mae Carlisle 1941-1944 and Una Mae Carlisle 1944-1950. If I had to choose just a song, nothing else, my all-time favorite might be Una Mae singing *Walkin' By the River*. Her husky voice coupled with lyrics suggesting a memorable tryst with her lover has mesmerized me for decades whenever I hear it. Recorded with the renowned Benny Carter on trumpet it is a classic of music and song in 1930s ballads. Born in 1907 Benny Carter is accomplished, distinctive and famous for his abilities on both trumpet and saxophone. Una Mae's recordings of *Now I Lay Me Down to Dream* and *I see a Million People* are no less memorable and alluring.

And then there is Ella Mae Morse. You haven't heard of her? You missed a legend. She was the queen of boogie-woogie, a form of jazz popular just before and during World War II. It was characterized by fast, bass-tone piano playing and Ella Mae was its poster girl. She sang the vocals of boogie-woogie better than anyone else. She had a relatively short career beginning in the early 1940s with the Freddie Slack orchestra who appeared only on the West Coast. Later she embarked on a solo career.

Boogie-woogie is difficult to describe unless you've listened to it but it's a "happy" music, one that makes you want to get up and dance. One felt good, forgot their worries and thought only about enjoying life when Morse sung *Cow Cow Boogie* or *Mr. Five by Five*. Several compact discs are available today by asking a music store to order them for you. Other "happy" songs by her were *Milkman Keep Those Bottles Quiet*, *Shoo Shoo Baby* and *The House of Blue Lights*. *Milkman* was a song about having to work a night shift in a war production plant and then coming home to get some sleep without too much disturbance by a noisy milkman. This may sound trite to you today but it wasn't in the World War II era. It was just the type of song to catch on with women working seven nights a week and needing some sleep in the morning, especially with a "happy" focus and Ella Mae's styling. As soon as she began singing, some part of one's body had to start moving. It was impossible to keep still. She was infectious!

The Count Basie band recorded the song *Boogie Woogie* in the late 1930s but it took World War II to make that musical genre popular and Ella Mae was its symbol. Many pianists adopted the style for a few years but she was the top vocalist. Servicemen in World War II loved boogie-woogie, not only because they loved listening to her, but because it was the most danceable swing music ever heard, a perfect music to jitterbug to, which was so popular at that time. Count Basie also recorded *Basie Boogie*, Gene Krupa, *Drumboogie*, Will Bradley and Ray McKinley, *Beat Me Daddy, Eight to the Bar* and *Scrub Me Mama With a Boogie Beat*, Johnny Mercer, *G.I. Jive* and Phil Harris, *Ain't Nobody Here But Us Chickens*, all boogie-woogie hits at one time. Obviously the song titles were as unique as the music.

After the war the boogie-woogie style seemed to fade. Ella Mae went on to rhythm-and-blues, even some pop ballads, but never had the success of the war years. Some say bebop, which also became popular in the 1940s, was an offshoot of boogie-woogie but bebop was rarely vocalized, usually instrumental, and seemed a musical form of its own. Perhaps she should be credited with the beginning of rock 'n' roll. Many of her songs seemed to fit that genre except the lyrics were understandable unlike most rock lyrics today.

I may have seen her perform in the early 1940s in Los Angeles where she played with the Freddie Slack band but I'm not certain. Those early war years in Los Angeles were chaotic. Night clubs abounded at beach communities but the town was dark outside and sometimes one wasn't certain where they were going or who they saw there. Favorite servicemen hangouts were clubs on Hermosa and Redondo Beaches, These were large ballrooms, not crowded during the war years, where good local bands like Freddie Slack appeared with popular singers like Ella Mae Morse. She continued her career until the mid-1950s when she retired to raise a family of six children and was forgotten by the music and jazz public. Boogie-woogie didn't survive long as a musical style but it was great while it lasted!

Freddie Slack and his band were perfect accompaniments to Ella Mae in those years. He wrote the songs and she sang them. Slack was a pianist, the heart of the boogie-woogie sound, who had been an arranger with several famous bands earlier in his career. After their success together, Freddie Slack went on to compose numerous other hit songs and his bands appeared in several musical movies in Hollywood in the 1940s but he was a West Coast prodigy and stayed there throughout his career, dying too soon in 1965 at the age of fifty-five.

I was in New York sometime in the late 1980s, staying at a midtown hotel, when I looked at the entertainment sheet for that evening in Manhattan and was surprised and excited to see the name of Ella Mae Morse premiered on the bill at a local club. When I called for reservations, I was informed her show had been cancelled an hour or two earlier. Apparently, at the last minute, she did not feel able to go on after a long absence from the stage and made a decision to not appear. It was one of my major entertainment disappointments. Ella Mae, born in 1924 (a popular year – Ella Mae, Sarah Vaughan and me), died in 1999 at the age of seventy-five. Incomparable as a stylist, she flashed across the jazz and blues scene like a bright star and was gone.

I also missed seeing Nat Cole live. In the 1980s I was fortunate to see his younger brother, Freddie Cole, in several personal appearances. If one shut their eyes, it was easy to hear some of Nat in Freddie's voice and style but Freddie has never attained Nat's popularity. In my opinion Nat had – and has – no peer in the male vocal world. Most music lovers are familiar with his vocals, legendary remembrances of soft, sentimental, expressive tales of love lost and love gained.

Casual fans may also forget that Nat Cole was one of the finest jazz pianists to ever perform. Early recordings of the King Cole Trio, in the late 1930s, where Nat was featured on the piano and as a vocalist, are priceless. His Trio always had great, great sidemen and they all blended together in those years, with Nat the star, singing and playing, to a perfection no other trio has ever reached. My favorite recording of the Trio is an old cassette I stumbled across many years ago, in a slush pile at a music store, called *Nat Cole Intimate*. It is the Trio recorded live at The Dew Drop Inn (now long defunct, I am told), in New Orleans in 1940. This recording, made by Frank Painiet, LaSalle St., New Orleans, and produced by The Deluxe Communications Corporation, New York, can best by described as sparkling. The Trio is at its best, Nat is superb on the piano and his mellow voice on *The Trouble With Me is You, Don't Cry, Cry Baby* and *Sweet Lorraine* is vintage Nat Cole. I believe I paid two dollars for this cassette. I wouldn't sell it now for two hundred!

The Cole family legacy also remains bright through the singing of Nat's daughter, Natalie Cole. Beset with problems much of her career (read her recent autobiography *Angel On My Shoulder*, a fascinating book) she has courageously overcome them and is today one of the premier artists in the popular ballad and soul world.

In fact, Natalie Cole has the unique ability – very unique today – to sing soul and rhythm and blues numbers and pronounce the lyrics so they are understandable. She came out with a new album in September 2002 that is awesome! I know that's an overused, somewhat trite, expression but no other describes the album so well. Several weeks before it was available, I was given a preview album with only four songs on it from the soon-to-be-released regular album. I played those four songs nightly. After a week I couldn't wait each evening to hear them again. When I finally received the full album, I gave the 4-song, promotional album to a friend with the admonition, "Play these each night for three nights in a row and you won't listen to anything else from that time on." Awesome? You bet!

There are some artists today who are superb entertainers but their number is very small unfortunately. Whether we were listening to big bands or small jazz combos in the 1930s, however, we always understood what they were singing or playing. It was a unique time in history. Life outside music was difficult in the Great Depression years and the sweet, sentimental, romantic songs of many entertainers were a welcome escape from the world of few jobs and little money. My high school yearbook published a poll of graduating seniors and reported Glen Miller was the favorite band. Female vocalist favorites were Dinah Shore, Martha Tilton and Helen O'Connel. Favorite male vocalists were Bob and Ray Eberle, Tex Beneke, Bing Crosby and Harry Babbitt, all on the "sweet" side.

After this adulation of 1930s music it is difficult to even mention today's popular sounds. There are currently a few appealing songs and I enjoy some "light rock" that features bands and singers dedicated to entertaining us and not deafening our sensibilities. I also appreciate other jazz "offshoots" like reggae. The only contemporary songs I can remember I have truly enjoyed are mostly from the 1980s, for example, *Hotel California,* by the Eagles, *One Less Bell to Answer,* The 5th Dimension, *Stuck on You,* Lionel Richie, *Reminiscing,* Little River Band, and *By the Time I Get to Phoenix,* by whomever has recorded it. That probably dates me but so be it!

In general, however, today's music has several deficiencies. It is loud, repetitive to a fault, buttressed by artists often performing hideous antics and with lyrics most often not fathomable as English. Added to these deficiencies are overt suggestions for violence and sex against often-maligned groups such as police, women and minorities. This crudeness and profanity was unknown in popular music of the 1930s.

Some philosophers will say you can judge the decay of a society by its morals. I agree with that but "morals" is a broad category. More specifically, I believe the hallmark is its music. I'm not so naïve as to believe we will all turn to the "oldies" for our musical entertainment but we can turn to some sanity and clarity, can we not?

The bobbysoxers of my era screamed their heads off for Frank Sinatra, and later The Beatles, but while they were going berserk over these celebrities you could understand the words the musicians were singing and discern a melody to the music. Rock or rap or heavy metal or hip-hop, or whatever its called today, is only a cacophony of sound laced with profanity, brutality and irreverence. That's noise, not music!

On September 30, 2002, the Minneapolis *Star Tribune* newspaper, in an editorial, no less, laudatory of recent performances of senior-aged rock stars, making their final tours in some instances, opined, "Rock 'n' roll requires considerably more energy than anything attempted by, say, Lawrence Welk or other past troubadours on the senior circuit." A writer of a "Letter to the editor" quickly responded to this editorial comment. He wrote, in part, "Tell that to Louis Armstrong, Duke Ellington, Jimmie Lunceford, or any other band leader of the '30s, '40s and '50s. The musicians in those bands blew their guts out night after night on one-night stands traveling around the country without any electronic help. They generated their own sound, acoustically. That takes a lot more energy than just plucking on an amplified guitar. It seems that, discounting acrobats, the only member of a rock band really working is the drummer." A good response and, I will add, "If you want to see acrobats, go to the circus."

Bands and band leaders like Basie, Armstrong and Lunceford, to name just a few, toured until they reached ages in the seventies to eighties. Most of their dates were one-night engagements and primarily in an era when racial discrimination caused them severe problems and limited their travel to buses, not private jets.

Charley Reese, syndicated columnist, framed the problem in the entertainment industry appropriately when he wrote for King Features Syndicate, Inc., in June, 2002, "The vulgarity, profanity and violence you see in entertainment are there only because those individuals occupying the position of power in the entertainment industry said 'Yes.' If they said 'No,' those things would disappear from the screens and the magazine racks. Our problem is that most of our elite have become corrupted. Many are nihilistic and hedonistic."

This decay in the music (and entertainment) industry will persist until distaste for it sickens the soul of the general population and a ground swell of opinion rises against it. Unlikely, yes, but this could begin with television viewers boycotting advertisers who use unsavory performers and promote salacious material. What have we to lose? Not much! And a whole world (of music) to gain, to enjoy, to appreciate.

Are there lessons to be learned from the Great Depression days? Yes, there are. There isn't anything wrong with something sweet or something sentimental, not hallmarks, unfortunately, of today's music. Maybe that's what we need to slow us down from this frantic pace in which so many of us are trapped that is becoming more intense, more chaotic as the years go by. Some new music, at least some new softer, cleaner styles in music, could provide that relief. Let us begin by boycotting advertisers who ignore these problems.

◆Chapter Seven: **RECREATION**

This is a difficult subject on which to draw contrasts as well as a subject that has its tenets in several activities discussed elsewhere in this book. It's tempting to say recreation or entertainment (and we will use those terms interchangeably) in the 1930s was less structured and more family oriented but that may be too broad an observation.

One obvious contrast, however, is the amount of time available. In the 1930s a forty-four hour work week was standard. Now a thirty-five to forty hour week is standard. Recreation and entertainment was also more "home-grown" in the 1930s. With no television I can remember reading, playing Monopoly, playing cards or some type of sports hour after hour. Movies were enormously popular and were the primary entertainment outside the home.

Another example of contrast is the influence of the automobile. Even if we lived in the same city all our lives it was routine in the 1930s to go for a ride on Sunday afternoon. The attraction of riding was undoubtedly enhanced by the emerging ownership of automobiles but most homes owned one auto by that time so that wasn't the sole answer. It was always attractive to pack the family in the automobile and drive around the parks or lakes or any place that had not been seen recently. It's difficult now to explain the rationale for this but the practice was taken for granted as a normal, frequent, pleasurable entertainment in those years. It was also inexpensive in an era when money was scare and the price of gas was in the ten-cent per gallon range. Today families rarely go for rides just for the sake of riding. There usually has to be some other reason for getting in an automobile.

After declining each year in the early 1930s, sales of automobiles picked up annually in the latter part of that decade and America's love with the vehicle was firmly established amid difficult economic conditions. Automobile design was emerging from a square, boxy shape, prevalent before 1930, to a more streamlined shape prominent in 1934. The auto industry at that time was forecasting future shapes that looked much like a chicken egg with the blunt end facing forward, about like a modern airplane fuselage without wings. Fortunately, this design never made it off the drawing boards of auto futurists!

Other opportunities for recreation were few in number. Little League games for young people, for example, were non-existent. There were more movie theaters but few legitimate theaters, very few large arenas and far fewer restaurants. In the 1930s people went to a restaurant because the housewife was sick or their schedule mandated it. Today restaurant visits are a form of entertainment and relaxation with the necessity of eating a secondary consideration.

A huge contrast, however, is television. In the 1930s there wasn't any. Now it permeates our society like a fog in inclement weather. No one would be so foolish as to state they wished television had never been invented. It has produced many hours of valuable news reporting, historical documentaries, comedies, motion pictures and sporting events. Conversely, it has produced an equal or greater number of hours of inane, violent, sexually offensive garbage unequalled from any other information or entertainment medium in the history of humanity. The Internet may surpass those dubious distinctions but the verdict is still out.

In my opinion, the bad in television overwhelms the good at this date. The tragic aspect to horrible television programming is that an entire generation of young people have grown up with this as their example of normal society and civilization. It's frightening to contemplate the trash that has been implanted in these young, impressionable minds as normal activities in which everyone engages.

The advent of cable has increased this problem. The original broadcast network was stilted in its variety but it exhibited some self-censorship. Today's cable stations demonstrate little censorship of violence, sex and offensive material. Censorship is the dirtiest of dirty words to the entertainment/broadcast industry but censorship in many forms is a part of our civilization and the rule of law. Unless we apply some of the dreaded "C" word to our television programming in the coming years, we will have produced successive generations of illiterate, violent, non-social idiots to populate and own this once great country named the United States of America.

Decay of a country comes from within, not from without, and the decadent parts of television can be, in fact, already are, the catalyst for this fall from glory. Someone once said, and I don't know who it was but we should be eternally grateful for his or her wisdom, "Civilization is a process of defining limits." Perhaps it was a Greek philosopher. They had wisdom we would be well to emulate twenty-five hundred years later. This dislike, this horror of anything resembling censorship is unfortunate. The absence of all censorship is anarchy: confusion, chaos and disorder. How we can be so frightened about setting standards, about making judgments, about declaring absolutes is both illogical and perilous to our democracy.

Radio was our opiate. The children were thrilled and seduced by *Jack Armstrong the All-American Boy, Tarzan, Adventures of Red Rider, Adventures of Tom Mix* and *The Cinnamon Bear.* Adults listened to *The Jack Benny Show, The Fred Allen Show, Myrt and Marge, Fibber McGee and Molly, Ma Perkins, The Eddie Cantor Show, The Little Theatre Off Times Square, The Major Bowes Amateur Hour,* and, probably, most popular of all, The Lucky Strike Cigarettes *Hit Parade.* The favorite national news announcer was the renowned H.V. Kaltenborn.

Here's one complete day on radio station WABC, New York, for Thursday, February 8, 1934, listed in the *New York Times* of that date. The programs may seem mundane to today's reader but to us they were interesting. Note the emphasis on music of all kinds, particularly popular dance orchestras.

7:30   A.M. Organ Reveille
8:00   Salon Musicale
9:00   Eton Boys Quartet
9:15   String Orch.
9:45   Mystery Chef
10:00   Bill and Ginger, Songs
10:15   Talk – Ida Bailey Allen
10:30   Melody Parade
11:00   Studio Music
11:30   Tony Wons; Keenan and Phillips – Piano Duo
11:45   A New Branch of Surgery – Dr. Howard
Lilienthal, Bellevue Hospital
12:00   Voice of Experience
12:15   P.M. – Connie Gates, Songs; Shuster Orch.
1:00   Marie, the Little French Princess – Sketch
1:15   Beauty Talk; Music
1:30   Easy Aces – Sketch
1:45   Dance Orch.
2:00   Ann Leaf
2:15   Romance of Helen Trent – Sketch
2:30   School of the Air
3:00   Metropolitan Orch.
3:30   National Student Federation Program
3:45   Curtis   Symphony   Orch.,   Fritz   Reiner,
Conductor
4:30   Madison Ensemble
4:45   Happy Minstrel
5:00   Skippy – Sketch
5:15   Hall Orch.
5:30   Jack Armstrong, All-American Boy – Sketch
5:45   Stamp Adventures Club – Sketch
6:00   Buck Rogers – Sketch
6:15   Bobby Benson – Sketch
6:30   Tito Guizar, Tenor
6:45   Little Italy – Sketch
7:00   Myrt and Marge
7:15   Just Plain Bill – Sketch
7:30   Serenaders Orch.

7:45   News – Boake Carter
8:00   Negro Quintet
8:15   News – Edwin C. Hill
8:30   Shilkret Orch; Alexander Gray, Songs; William Lyons Phelps, Narrator
9:00   Philadelphia Orch.; Sylvan Levin, Conductor
9:15   Howard March, Tenor; Mary Eastman, Soprano: Kostelanets Orch.
9:30   Waring Orch.; Fray & Braggiotti, Piano Duo
10:00 Gray Orch; Irene Taylor, songs
10:30 Premiers, Opera – Four Saints in Three Acts, Athenaeum, Hartford
10:45 News Bulletins
11:00 California Melodies
11:30 James Orch.
12:00 Nelson Orch.
12:30 A.M. – Lyman Orch.
1:00   Pancho Orch.

People also read a lot. Each city had several newspapers, both morning and evening editions, and lots of magazines. A good selection of new books was published regularly. In one week in 1934 newly published titles in the *New York Times* were: *The Making of Americans*, by Gertrude Stein (Harcourt, Brace, $3), *The American Adventure*, by John Bonn (Day, $2.50), *An Introduction to Logic and Scientific Method*, by Morris R. Cohen and Ernest Nagel (Harcourt, Brace, $3.50), *I Know Just the Thing for That*! by J.F. Montague (Day, $2), *Seaplane Solo*, by Francis Chichester (Harcourt, Brace, $2.50), *Mr. Zouch: Superman*, by Anthony Powell (Vanguard, $2), and *How to Succeed in Life*, by Grenville Kleiser (Funk & Wagnalls, $2). Those prices may look like a bargain today but not in 1934.

The contrast between today's society dominated by the influence of television and the homebred society of the 1930s is calculably in favor of the latter. If we went out for entertainment, it was to the movies. Three themes dominated: love stories, comedies and musicals. Examples were *Animal Crackers, Duck Soup* and *Horse Feathers* with the Marx Brothers, *Mutiny on the Bounty, Mr. Deeds*

Goes to Town, The Great Ziegfeld, Boys Town and, of course, *Gone with the Wind*. The sex and violence of today was non-existent.

In the early 1940s one of the most entertaining movies ever made, *Song of the South*, was released. After discharge from World War II service I had a part time job checking attendance at movie theaters for a local film distributor. At one theater I saw this movie eight or nine times in a three-day stretch. The story line and music were infectious. It got better each time I viewed it. I could barely keep my attention on recording ticket buyers.

Unfortunately, the plot and story were protested by some groups as representing slavery favorably. This was absurd. The story, a combination of animation and live actors, portrayed a young white boy who ran away from home and wound up in the care of a former slave who teaches him some valuable lessons in life his parents should have taught him. What really makes the movie remarkable is the accompanying music with songs the viewer will leave the theater humming for days if not years. When I am asked, "What is your favorite movie of all time?" I immediately reply, "*Song of the South.*" It had the rare – very rare – advantage of a movie that both appealed and was suitable for children of all ages and adults.

Unfortunately, this movie, a classic example of the wholesomeness of that era, has never been re-released by the company holding its copyright.

I was recently given two free passes, valid for six months, to a local motion picture theater, one of those multiple screen theaters that offer twelve or thirteen movies simultaneously. Not being an avid movie fan I glanced occasionally in the newspaper to see what movies they were playing. For several months I found nothing of interest, even for free! Finally, as the six months was expiring, I searched the movie guide of that theater every week to try and find something I could tolerate. The last week, with my wife, we went to the theater hoping to look at the billboards displayed there to see if something might be worthwhile. When we handed our free passes to the ticket man at a desk in the lobby, he said, "What movie do you want to see?" We said, "We don't know yet. We'd like to look at the billboards in the lobby to find something." He was obviously taken aback. Apparently he had never had this request. He was kind enough, however, and, given our advanced age, said, smiling, "Okay, go on in.

Look around. Then come back and tell me what you want." His charity was probably not as magnanimous as it seemed because he knew we were on passes and there was no hard cash at stake but, nevertheless, the problem was resolved. We finally found one movie, a nineteenth century British comedy, but left in the middle of it because we couldn't make out what the actors were saying half the time.

Before you judge us as hopeless elders, completely out of touch with the world, let me hasten to add my favorite television series, or sitcom to use that awful word, is *As Time Goes By*, a British comedy, no less, that began playing in the early 1990s.

I have the first forty episodes and will purchase more as soon as they are released. The plot line is intriguing but not remarkable. A young British officer meets and falls in love with a nurse before going off to the Korean War. He writes to her but the letter is lost so she believes he no longer cares about her. Because he receives no reply, he believes she has lost interest in him so never writes to her again. After marriages by both parties that ultimately leave them widow and widower they meet by chance forty years later, resume the courtship and ultimately marry. What makes this series so delightful is not that plot but the acting of two very talented individuals. The incomparable Judi Dench, lovable, sexy and transfixing (at any age), plays the woman in the play, Jean Pargetter, and Geoffrey Palmer, a stoic, dry wit, but gallant and cuddly, is Lionel Hardcastle, the male lead.

One must sit up close to hear all the dialogue but it is worth the effort. Jean lets no bit of sarcasm or effrontery go by without an equal or better response and Lionel is so understated and laid back, but yet so witty, one chuckles or laughs continuously while watching. After forty years Jean and Lionel develop a love that is tender and engrossing but with the rare ability few relationships possess to allow a challenge to one another whenever they disagree. Then, after a marvelous bit of dialogue or verbal spat, they settle their differences, usually humorously, and the bond between them strengthens. All couples should have this ability. It would enhance every relationship while adding spice to each moment.

This is not British slapstick, by the way, of which there is far too much. This is British humor at its best and most seductive. If only we could have more of this entertainment in United States television and less violence and stupidity.

In the 1930s local college football was our passion. The entire State of Minnesota paused on Saturday afternoons in the fall months and listened to the games broadcast on radio from Memorial Stadium on the University of Minnesota campus. The Golden Gophers, as the football team was named, won four national championships and six Big Ten championships in that decade. Their coach was a no-nonsense, strict disciplinarian named Bernie Bierman, now a legend at the school. Players were alternately afraid and inspired by Bierman, rare qualities in coaches today.

Two-platoon football had not made its debut and most of the players played on both offense and defense. As we listened to the broadcasts and read about the team in the newspapers we became familiar with the names of all the players. We cheered and agonized over the play-by-play reports as they came to us, huddled around our one radio in the living room. At the beginning of the broadcast, at timely spots throughout the broadcast, and after each "Gophers" touchdown, we heard the marching band at the game play *The Minnesota Rouser*. A peppy, spirited, rah! rah! tune, it made everyone listening on radio, and presumably all in attendance at the game, tremendously excited.

In succeeding decades, as problems and scandals at the University of Minnesota escalated, and the football team moved their games to a sterile, antiseptic bubble stadium in downtown Minneapolis known as the Metrodome, my allegiance to the University's athletics waned, despite my graduation from that school. Consequently, I had not been to one of their athletic events for a long, long time. Several months ago, however, I attended a Minnesota Women's Hockey game. As the team came on to the ice to start the game, the band played *The Minnesota Rouser* that I had not heard for many years. To my surprise a tingling sensation ran up and down my spine as I stood and cheered those women skating on to the ice and the feeling stayed with me until the *Rouser* was over. I felt like I was back in 1934 at the age of ten huddled around that radio listening to "my team, my idols," score a touchdown to win the game with, perhaps, a national championship hanging in the balance.

That was our world, how we thought and who we looked up to, in the Great Depression years. Some bad years, yes, but, oh, so many good, honest years, so many uplifting memories from a time when simple pleasures filled our lives.

After movies and football the national pastime was baseball, primarily professional baseball. There were only sixteen major league teams, eight American League and eight National League. Supporting these were approximately four hundred minor league teams, a few independently owned and operated but the majority affiliates of a major league team. Players advanced to the major league by playing first on a class D minor league team, then to C, B, A, double A and finally triple A. If they made it to the major leagues, they were well-grounded in baseball's fundamentals, unlike players today who jump from a college campus to an A team and then expect to be promoted to the American or National League in one or two years.

Today the D, C and B teams are long gone. Part of this is grade creep (like school grades) but with thirty major league teams in the American and National Leagues combined, nobody wants to tarry in the minors and few cities will provide support for teams of that classification. The fans see a steady diet of major league games on television so why support anything less in their own backyard? Minor leagues used to be geographically aligned and close together so natural rivalries were born. Today the Pacific Coast League, believe it or not, consists of teams from Des Moines, Iowa; Omaha, Nebraska; New Orleans, Louisiana; Memphis, Tennessee and Canada to augment their California, Oregon and Washington cities. How can a team from Portland, Oregon feel any rivalry with a team from Memphis, Tennessee? Unbelievable!

In Minneapolis, in the 1930s, we cheered our home team, win or lose, in a ballpark seating five thousand fans, many of those in back of pillars and posts, and had a ball (excuse the pun). We saw Ted Williams and, later, Willie Mays, two of the greatest players in the history of the game, play for the Millers, as the team was called, on their way to the Boston Red Sox and New York Giants respectively. We thoroughly enjoyed every daytime game in the warm sunshine. Night games, which came later, never had the same appeal.

Ted Williams was on the Minneapolis Millers team in 1938 before being called up by the Boston Red Sox. He was a tempestuous character even in those early years. As a nineteen-year-old with the Millers he became as well known for his temper as his hitting (which was phenomenal). Willie Mays did not come to the Millers until 1951. After appearing in just thirty-five games and hitting .477, the New York Giants could wait no longer and called him up before most Minneapolis fans had a chance to see him perform.

The Minneapolis Millers and St. Paul Saints, our hated rival across the Mississippi River, were a mixture of rookies on the way up to the major leagues and aging veterans, who wouldn't give up the game, on their way down. It was a wonderful era in the national pastime, one never to be repeated. Today the players are larger and stronger but their skill level has declined markedly. Tell this to a young person today and their initial rebuttal is how many home runs so-and-so hits in a year. That's easy with a reduced strike zone, an umpire who protects the batter from even a brush-off pitch and a juiced up baseball that jumps off the bat like a golf ball. Ball manufacturers will deny a livelier ball but how else can a one hundred and sixty-pound batter take a feeble swing at a baseball on the outside of the plate and watch it disappear over the fence?

The all-time travesty is some of these domed stadiums with artificial turf where the baseball bounces like a tennis ball when it hits the "ground." I don't know what that game is called but it's not baseball.

But it was real baseball in the 1930s. The Minneapolis Millers had unique players like Joe Hauser, a prodigious home run hitter, who hit sixty-nine in 1933, Ab Wright, an all-around "slugger" (home runs, hits, runs-batted-in) for many years, Jess Petty, a pitcher who, in his late thirties, won almost twenty games in each of three seasons, "Broadway" Charlie Wagner, a twenty-game wining pitcher, so named for his handsome looks and impeccable wardrobe, and Spencer Harris, a graceful, speedy centerfielder who played for ten years for the Millers, compiling several minor-league records, and finally finished his career in his late forties in the Pacific Coast League.

My stepmother was a good baseball fan and when I was very young, six or seven years old, she would frequently sit with me in the summer afternoons in the living room listening to Halsey Hall announce the Miller's games. Halsey had a melodious voice and soothing style that, beginning in 1933, endeared him to Minnesota sports fans for decades. His trademark expression was "Holy Cow," a momentous pronouncement when Halsey Hall uttered it after some unusual event on the field. He was a legend in Minnesota sports announcing and people of my age, and many younger, remember him with reverence and fondness.

I didn't realize it at the time but in later years I learned that some of the early baseball broadcasts on radio, when the home team was playing in another city, were accomplished by an announcer sitting and reading a paper tape telegraph feed from the town where the game was played. This announcer would add his own interpretations to the sparse facts on the tape. For example, if the tape read, "Ball one, ball two, single to right," the local announcer would announce it as, "The pitcher delivers, ball one. The next pitch is on its way, high and ball two. The pitcher is ready, here's the pitch, (the batter) swings and it's a line drive to right field, (the batter) stops at first."

We didn't have much in those years but we made the most of what was available even if a bit of deceit was employed on occasion.

When I have the opportunity today I travel a few miles to a small town – any town – in Minnesota and watch the amateur town team on Sunday afternoon. This is fun! The players, who have regular jobs during the week, are enthusiastic, even if their skill level has diminished, the fans are in to the game every inning (they don't come there to eat) and most of them know an infield fly rule when they see it.

The best example I can give you of the difference between professional baseball when I was young and today is an anecdote about Ted Williams who died recently, in July of 2002. *The San Diego Union-Tribune* newspaper, in an article about his death on July 6, 2002, quoted the following comment from Bob Breitbard, Williams' lifelong friend. Breitbard said he and Williams had almost daily phone chats the past twenty years and Williams would say to Breitbard every time he ended their chat, "I love you, my dear friend."

That's an example of friendship and devotion from one of the most respected and famous and skilled players in the world, one who came into baseball in its renowned years of the 1930s, one who gave some of the best playing years of his life to the service of this country as a combat pilot in World War II, one who was a man among men, but who knew the value of loyal friends and was not afraid to express his emotions to those friends.

As disgusting as are some of the sexual tete-a-tetes on television the real damage being done to young peoples minds and morals is from the horrible, explicit, nauseating examples of violence on display every day. These examples, many showing the utter depravity of mankind, are bound to desensitize and confuse the minds of young people who should be growing up with better examples by which to live and view the world.

The prospect for any improvement in the quality of our entertainment and recreation is similar to the previous category of music: We will need a groundswell of public opinion, disgusted with the status quo, to harass and boycott advertisers until they sponsor less offensive fare.

While this may be unlikely, think of the consequences if we don't do it. This book is based on the premise there may be some lessons in history that, if we adopt them, will improve our present society. Isn't higher quality entertainment and recreation one of those possibilities? I believe it is so let us start that "groundswell" now and see if it will grow. There is nothing to lose and a country to gain. Five stars for entertainment and recreation in the 1930s. No stars for today.

Are there lessons to be learned from the Great Depression days? Obviously, there are. Recreation and entertainment cry out for reform. It can be done. Changes are possible beginning with boycotts of advertisers. Do we have the will to do it? I hope so!

♦Chapter Eight: **GOVERNMENT**

The 1930s government was markedly less intrusive in the lives of its citizens than today's government. Even at the height of the Great Depression, with thirty to forty percent unemployment, government was less visible. The NRA, or National Recovery Act, which was designed to lift the country out of the depression, lasted only two years. Authorized in 1933 to stimulate competition and place a seal of approval on compliant products the NRA was declared unconstitutional in 1935. Now, in the twenty-first century, we have food stamps, welfare, agricultural subsidies, empowerment districts, corporate bailouts, multiple layers of taxes and hundreds of other programs resonating, in multiple ways, throughout our lives.

Most visibly, there were fewer cops on the street in the 1930s. Objectors to this assertion might point to statistics that suggest the number of cops per thousand citizens was higher in the 1930s but they forget the hordes of law enforcement people who back up the current police. These include, but are not limited to, local detectives, the FBI, INS, DNR, ATF, Postal Inspectors and multitudes of other enforcement personnel that direct environmental laws, food and drug inspections and similar activities. The cops we did see in the 1930s were primarily on foot, "walking a beat." A cop on foot is reassuring to the neighborhood. Unfortunately, in many neighborhoods today, that beat cop would be nothing more than a good target. Modern police need the protection and mobility of an automobile to function with any efficiency and safety.

That is a telling contrast between the two periods: We can no longer support peace officers on foot because it is too dangerous. All the contrasts I might draw are not as persuasive as this one. There are intensely crowded downtown areas in major cities where this doesn't apply because of choking traffic conditions but throughout the country cops on foot are a forgotten breed.

Another visible sign of government today is the multitude of traffic lights and stop signs in all parts of every city. The fact they're needed is not the question. The question is how numerous they are. In the 1930s, in Minneapolis and St. Paul at least, and probably in many other cities, the only street signal was a square post that was anchored to the middle of the intersection. It was approximately four feet high and inside the post was a square, revolving fixture that had the word GO affixed on two opposite sides and illuminated in green. The word STOP was affixed on the other two sides of the square and illuminated in red. It was electrically controlled so traffic going north or south, for example, would see a signal to GO while, simultaneously, traffic going east or west would see a signal to STOP.

Placed in the middle of the street it presented a handy target for careless motorists to bump into and was a special obstruction for motorists making a left turn. City workers were constantly replacing and repairing these signs. They suffered a high rate of damage.

At other places in the streets motorists were responsible for watching out for themselves. There were signs regulating speed and cautioning the presence of school children and other restrictions but nowhere near the innumerable signage of today. As a result, today's signs are frequently ignored by motorists who have become both offended and sanitized by their proliferation. Anyone who doubts this should ask themselves how many motorists obey speed laws anywhere in this country. The answer, if you're honest, is very few.

I don't believe there is any contrast, however, as prominent as the contrast in taxation. This is a subject that could fill volumes with statistics and prove any point this writer was trying to prove but let's begin by identifying, in Minnesota at least, the taxes we did not have in the 1930s that are commonplace now. We did not have a sales tax, a state income tax (except for the very wealthy), a fishing license tax (or even a fishing license), or a tax to own a rowboat, for example. The taxes or license fees on all other items, i.e., automobiles, gas, real estate and on and on, ad infinitum, were a fraction of today's tax rate. A driver's license was obtained by filling out a short application and paying less than fifty cents as I remember. No other examinations were required like visual, behind-the-wheel, etc.

Sales taxes in Minneapolis entertainment venues (bars, clubs, etc.) now total twelve and one-half percent. That rate is achieved by a six and one-half percent statewide sales tax, a one-half percent city tax and five and one-half percent special tax levied on a convoluted basis and scale, depending on the venue and the product sold, for the remaining amount. The five and one-half percent was passed by the Minneapolis City Council several years ago to assist paying for a convention center immeasurably larger in size than a city of under one-half million people would ever warrant.

The scheme of tax withholding has immunized taxpayers to the point they do not realize the high rates they are paying. They look at the net pay on their paycheck after all taxes and other charges and recognize that as the significant amount.

The average middle-class wage earner today is paying close to fifty percent of their wages in taxes when they are finished paying them for the year, euphemistically speaking, some time in late May. This fifty percent estimate includes federal, state, local, sales, property, gasoline, and multitudes of excise taxes not to mention social security taxes which some would say are not "taxes" but surely have that name and effect pinned to them.

"Isn't that enough?" one would like to occasionally ask the politicians (or shout at them), but their insatiable appetite for more apparently says, "No."

Let me hasten to add, don't blame the politicians for this sorry state of affairs. They are only following a course that the voters reaffirm for them each election. If the public doesn't want, or doesn't object, to high taxation, the politicians will continue to be more than happy to spend their money with ever increasing glee. Cradle to grave government is what we "enjoy" in rapidly escalating amounts and that is what we will continue to have if the voters give it their stamp of approval at each election. This trend, to a government that provides all our needs, is responsible for our excessive level of taxation. Syndicated columnist for 2002 King Features Syndicate, Inc., Charley Reese, said it best in his column on March 6, 2002, "What we have is a semi-free, semi-socialistic society that is moving ever toward less freedom and more government control. Out of 535 members of the United States House and Senate, I doubt if you could find 50 who are ideologically either left or right. Most of them are just opportunists who wouldn't know a political philosophy if one crawled in bed with them."

If you don't believe taxes make a huge difference in the decisions of people and business, consider what has happened to automobile dealers in the city of Minneapolis. Twenty years ago new and used car dealers lined the main streets of the city. Then a half-percent city sales tax was added. Subsequently, new car dealers fled the city except one, a dealer selling cars at a range where price is not a factor. The reason: The city sales tax of one-half percent (on autos as well as everything else) is significant to most people about to make a buying decision. One-half percent of twenty-five thousand dollars is one hundred and twenty-five dollars. Why pay that to the government after dickering for an hour with an auto salesperson over a few hundred dollars on the purchase price?

Are we providing better care and support to the poor and disadvantaged today than we were in the 1930s? Probably, yes. But in our zeal to do this we have overcompensated to a huge degree and millions of middle-income people in this country believe government benefits, grants and subsidies are their unalterable right as citizens. They view the government as a bottomless pit of largess with no recognition that their gifts come from their fellow taxpayers.

Compounding this situation is the problem that all levels of government rarely make decisions with the best interest of their citizens foremost in mind. Rather they make decisions based on what they perceive will make them "look good" which usually benefits a very narrow but influential segment of their constituency. No better example of this exists than the decision to build a light rail line in Minneapolis. A person would be a fool to deny that light rail, in some form, plays a significant role in the solution to traffic congestion and especially in the Twin Cities of Minneapolis and St. Paul who are presently choking on a roadway system totally inadequate for their size and growth profile.

So what did the legislators do? They approved a route for the initial leg of this system that has the least potential to alleviate auto traffic congestion. For people unfamiliar with the Twin Cities a geography lesson is necessary. The Twin Cities have a freeway ring route that encircles both cities. It's not much of a "freeway" because in most areas it is only two lanes in each direction. The congestion today, the stop-and-go condition at any hour, rivals some of the worst traffic areas in West Coast and East Coast cities many of which presently have several lanes, some as high as six, in each direction.

Is it too difficult a stretch to reason that if you want to relieve automobile congestion, you build alternative modes of transportation where the congestion is now? I would think not but it was for the legislators, i.e., politicians in this area. The City of Minneapolis is a behemoth in influence in the area. Consequently the first leg of the route will run from downtown Minneapolis, through mostly poor to lower-middle-class neighborhoods with frequent stops in these areas, to the regional airport and terminating at the ubiquitous Mall of America. The only automobile traffic this will eliminate is a few taxicab trips from the airport to downtown Minneapolis, and a few charter buses from the airport to the Mall of America. Residents along the light rail route in Minneapolis already take the bus to work. They do not drive downtown and pay eight to ten dollars or more per day to park an automobile. Thus they will continue using the bus with the possible exception of a few of them who live in close proximity to a light rail station. The few bus riders who switch to light rail will only increase the pressure for more subsidization to the existing bus system, presently operating, of course, at a loss.

The dirty little secret here is almost all forms of public transportation are money losers except roadways. Yes, roadways require some maintenance and upkeep but I believe that sum is far less per person, per passenger, per automobile, per capita, per mile, or any other measurement that can be concocted, than public transit systems.

So what's the purpose of this heavily subsidized project? The answer is simple. It's a neighborhood revitalization program for the areas it goes through in the City of Minneapolis, more social tinkering with what should be economic decisions. Construction at each stop has already attracted new investment in those areas despite the few riders that will ever enter or exit it. When it begins operation in 2004, annual operating costs are estimated to be twelve million dollars. Four million are estimated from rider fares, six million from the State of Minnesota and two to three million from the Federal Government and these are estimates made in a climate necessary to convince skeptics prior to the approval for funding. Guess how accurate they are!

Meanwhile the drivers in cars out on the two-lane "freeway" continue to inch ahead at five miles an hour or less and the cost for lost time and gasoline reaches astronomical proportions.

Solve a problem? Do it logically? Not in this town!

Myriad other schemes exist, most of them tax schemes. Their design is usually complicated so they're not understood by the average taxpayer. A prime example is a law in Minnesota called fiscal disparities. Passed in 1975 it mandates that all cities, suburbs and communities in the Minneapolis-St. Paul metropolitan area, almost two hundred in number, contribute forty percent of their growth in commercial tax base each year to a pool. Some formula is then used to establish an average growth rate in the tax base and those communities below that average divide up the funds in the pool. The communities above that average, who have attracted and accommodated new business, receive a net zero from the pool. This is an over simplification of the workings of this scheme but it is basically what happens when all the machinations of this robbery are completed. The suburb in which I live, one that attracts and accommodates new business investment, lost – and that's the operative word, lost – fifteen million dollars last year to this pool. Few people understand this scheme so it continues unabated but the worst aspect of it is that communities who gain the tax revenue love the scheme, have it built into their budget each year and will fight to the death to see it continue uninterrupted.

Even more onerous, if this is possible, is the progressiveness of our income tax systems. In the year 2000 the top one percent of taxpayers paid thirty-seven percent of the total income tax collected and the top five percent paid fifty-six percent. The top twenty-five percent paid eighty-four percent of the tax. The bottom fifty percent paid 3.9 percent (less than four percent). How much more progressive is fair?

Tossing aside the possibility that fairness might ever be a factor, consider the cry from the politicians whenever a tax cut is discussed that the plan "favors only the rich." If a tax cut is to have any impact, it has to be a tax cut on the fifty percent that pay almost all the tax, presumably "the rich." Cutting the taxes of taxpayers who pay almost no taxes wouldn't be much of a tax cut.

Think about this next time the question is debated. Don't just listen to someone promoting class warfare, THINK for yourself!

Less you believe I'm prejudiced for rich over poor I see no excuse for numerous tax breaks and subsidization that go to corporations and an equal abhorrence for high subsidies to agricultural interests that do nothing to solve agricultural problems except enrich large, already affluent farmers and encourage overproduction of surplus commodities. Our system is distorted in a number of directions that cry out for remedy. Looking back at the 1930s gives us glimpses of some better parameters.

We didn't have much money in the 1930s but we didn't pay high taxes on what we had. Easy as it is to make this a political contrast, I don't believe it's enough to frame it in those terms. High taxes are a social choice. Do we want a society based on today's tax system, rapidly running to confiscation, that attempts to provide everyone with all their needs, or do we want a society where the government provides for those citizens in urgent need but allows the remainder to get rich or remain middle class – or even remain poor – if that is their choice?

There is another danger to our country, growing in intensity each day. It is the raucous, virulent, malicious demonizing of candidates for public office that don't fit every interest group's profile. Llewellyn King, CEO of the *King Publishing Group* and Editor of *White House Weekly*, put it best in an article distributed by Knight Ridder News Service, published in the *St. Paul Pioneer-Press* newspaper on March 21, 2002, that said, "Over the past 30 years, both the electoral process and the presidential appointments process have become so ugly that one of the questions that should be asked of candidates and nominees is: What is wrong with you that you would subject yourself to this? For this reason the talent deficit in Washington grows with each administration, as the confirmation process worsens and the caliber of high government officers declines."

We need to find a better way to operate our government.

Continuing to weigh heavily on all we do – or don't do – is our current hang-up with the doctrine of separation of church and state. In addition to taking this "principle" to extreme conclusions, we are allowing it to eradicate all vestiges of religion from our schools and workplaces to the extent any mention, however innocuous, with the remotest connotation to a religious figure, is branded a scurrilous act.

The First Amendment, lest we forget, reads, "Congress shall make no law respecting an establishment of religion, or prohibiting the free exercise thereof; or abridging the freedom of speech, or of the press, or the right of the people peaceably to assemble, and to petition the Government for a redress of grievances." A book just published by the Harvard University Press, authored by Philip Hamburger, titled *Separation of Church and State*, looks critically at the current inflexibility of the interpretation of this Amendment. The author points out, as reported in a review of the book by Stephen Prothero in the July 30, 2002, *Wall Street Journal*, "The phrase (wall of separation) has become such a mantra that most Americans think it is enshrined in the Constitution, whereas the First Amendment proscribes only the federal establishment of religion and laws restricting its free exercise." Prothero's review further declares, "(This book) is delightfully iconoclastic, a great read that transforms a cherished belief of American civil religion into a myth."

Citizens are losing confidence in their government, whether city, state or federal. The accounting systems of the government make the corporate accounting scandals of 2001 and 2002 look benign. Who has any understanding of where surplus social security taxes go and where they are spent? The myth of a reserve fund someplace holding the surplus for later years backed by government securities is laughable. The government prints our money, prints the securities and effectively accounts to no one.

Ask your senator or representative sometime if there is a vault or bank or any place where you, a citizen of the country, can go and view this horde of securities supposedly backing up the social securities "trust" fund. What a misnomer!

What's backing it up is our faith in the ability or the will of politicians in future years to increase our taxes at that time to equal future requirements of the social security system (and the willingness and ability of we the citizens to pay those taxes). The actual forward-looking deficit of this country, or under-funded liability, is in the trillions of dollars and backed by only one factor: the concept that all of the citizens are naïve enough to consent to this Ponzi scheme and perpetuate its continuation.

Other government deceptions abound. Numerous government obligations are tied to the consumer price index or CPI, also called the cost-of-living index, so it is beneficial for the government to keep it as low as possible. In past years when the federal Bureau of Labor Statistics has announced a yearly CPI of, for example, two percent, everyone other than an idiot knows prices have increased from two to five times that percent. This CPI is ostensibly based on a market basket of goods and services that are supposed to be representative of those purchased by the average consumer. When questioned, which they rarely are, on the disparity between the announced CPI rate and the rate perceived to have taken place in the real world, the bureaucrats actually have the gall to offer this explanation: They have substituted hamburger for steak in one component of the index because the majority of citizens are now buying hamburger who can no longer afford steak.

Similarly ludicrous explanations will be offered for other components of the index. The most common absurdity is to make the statement that "core" inflation has only risen some modest amount. "Core" inflation, if you don't know its definition, is minus the components of food and energy. That's about like saying we don't have a crime problem if we subtract from the statistics the number of murders and robberies committed. These deceptions are worse than ludicrous. They are a purposeful attempt to deceive the public for the benefit of the politicians. Occasionally these absurdities will be examined in some Congressional hearing after a few voters have complained bitterly to their senator or representative about them. This travesty of logic will then be sincerely questioned and "examined" by grown men and women in one of their hearings where individual showboating takes precedence over any attempt to discover the truth.

Waste is endemic in government. Scratch the surface, assign some auditors to most any department, and you'll find massive abuses of discretionary spending. In 2003, when the State of Minnesota was faced with historic deficits, most departments were pleading for larger budgets. "Let someone else cut back," they cried in unison. Within one month investigative reporting by two television stations shone the light on massive expenditures for non-essential items that could easily have allowed them to cut their budget if they had been worthwhile stewards of the public funds (taxes) under their jurisdiction. We must reign in these excesses but sheer size is a problem. Who can corral these monoliths of government largess?

Correspondingly, if anyone doubts the comical aspect of the majority of legislative deliberations that subsequently affect them every day of their lives, they should attend some committee hearings when their state legislature is in session. Yes, on occasion, some laws are passed, or fortunately not passed, that are necessary and may, ultimately, bring us all some benefit but the vast majority of these committee deliberations are laughable. Numerous committee members are absent, are joking or talking with each other, and know very little about the subject being discussed. They will probably vote at some point on the advice or at the direction of their political party leader or from their own preconceived attitude gleaned from their constituent political base. The overriding merits or demerits of the subject under consideration are usually a secondary consideration.

One of the biggest jokes to these hearings is the frequently expressed request on the part of politicians to their voters to "get involved, come and testify. Tell us what you think." Prospective participants should know that citizen testimony in the vast majority of hearings is a waste of time unless one has formed an acquaintance with one or more members of the committee in advance of their testimony and that legislator has indicated a willingness to educate, influence or pressure some of their colleagues to follow what you are proposing. Legislators are no different than the average citizen. No matter their oath to represent all the public, they prefer to listen, talk and work with their own kind – other legislators – and not be bothered with the messy, unpredictable public.

Consequently, the process of passing new laws is the most unpredictable, untidy process imaginable and it will remain so as government grows and has an increasing amount of money to squander. There is a direct correlation between size and confusion in this process and it grows apace.

I have an example of how sheer size is a problem. I was executive director of a national association that ceased business in 1992. In August of that year we filed a certificate of dissolution with the state in which we had incorporated twenty years earlier. The name of the state is not important. It is one of several state governments along the Eastern seaboard all equally incompetent and derelict in serving the needs of their citizens and taxpayers. Within the first year of our application for dissolution representatives of this state told me we had never been incorporated (so could not be dissolved), lost my original incorporation papers which they then demanded I forward to them, lost a postal money order to cover the dissolution filing fee, lost the original dissolution filing papers and numerous supporting documents so the entire mess had to be replaced and, finally, failed to respond to dozens of phone calls in an effort to resolve these mishaps.

In August, 1994, after one more year of frustration and two years after the original filing, I received a certificate of dissolution dated, inexplicably, three months earlier, May 19, 1994. Periodically, during these two years, I would reach some sympathetic soul at a nearby desk or department to the one I was calling and be told, "(So and so) has stacks of correspondence several feet high on (his or her) desk. I haven't seen (him or her) for days. Don't know what to tell you. The supervisor isn't around either!"

I know these experiences are common, and some far worse, but it's the cavalier attitude, almost disdain, that some government employees exhibit to their constituents that is difficult to accept. Are there efficient, helpful government employees? Of course, and, fortunately, probably the majority, but there is a huge, huge minority who are worthless and this minority grows in size as overall government grows and becomes more complex and unmanageable.

What is the legitimate role for government in our society? It is not confined to good intentions. John Stuart Mill, English philosopher and economist, said it best in his essay, *On Liberty*, in 1851, reprinted in the book *The Clash of Political Ideals*, by Albert R. Chandler, and published by D. Appleton-Century Company. Mill said, "...that the sole end for which mankind are warranted, individually or collectively, in interfering with the liberty of action of any of their number, is self-protection. That the only purpose for which power can be rightfully exercised over any member of a civilized community, against his will, is to prevent harm to others. His own good, either physical or moral, is not a sufficient warrant." In Mill's day, only one hundred and fifty years ago, this principle was thought to be mildly revolutionary. Ponder how far we've moved away from that today.

But no matter, below this morass of good intentions, I believe, "The American people hunger for a statesman magnetized by the truth, unwilling to give up his good name, uninterested in calculation only for the sake of victory, unable to put his interests before those of the nation." That's a quote from an article by Mark Helprin in the *Wall Street Journal* on July 2, 1998, titled *Statesmanship and Its Betrayal*. Only when that man or woman comes along will this country reverse course and change its march to perdition. Winston Churchill was such a man. American history has many others.

One of these was a man named Joe Foss. Born in South Dakota in 1915 he became one of the greatest fighter pilots of all time. In the early months of World War II, when the United States was reeling from the blow dealt by Japan at Pearl Harbor, and our military was hanging on by its teeth all over the Pacific Ocean, Joe Foss, a marine fighter pilot, shot down twenty-six enemy planes over Guadalcanal. Subsequently awarded the Distinguished Flying Cross, the Bronze Star, the Silver Star and a Purple Heart, he went on to have a distinguished civilian career, most notably as governor of South Dakota from 1954 to 1958.

In a wide-ranging, "shoot-from-the-hip," interview with *The American Legion Magazine* just before his death in January of 2003, and published in its February, 2003 issue, one of the questions Joe Foss was asked was, "Why did you get into politics?" He replied, "Politics is the housekeeping of good government. I advise folks in the military service to get into politics because somebody who is ready to lay their life down for their country qualifies more than those you see there now. They're always greasing up something to pass for their local communities instead of looking out for the whole country."

In this advertising-mad world politicians count on public indifference to their performance to guarantee their re-election, term after term. They spend huge sums of money to bombard citizens with slanted or misleading ads before each election on the premise that if one hears, "Senator X is fighting for you every day," they'll believe it, not the first time but the one-hundredths time. Some of the real shouters and screamers make it sound like they're fighting for every known malady that exists, as if you lived in the jungle. This is not a third-world country. It's the United States of America. They treat you like robots that can be programmed to vote for them and you respond like robots. Wake up! Start thinking for yourself about what your country needs, not just your own welfare.

Illustrative of the "robot" theory, from my view, is a speech in Minneapolis on October 29, 2002, of a candidate for public office, that "brought the standing room-only crowd of more than 800 to its feet repeatedly," as reported the following day in the Minneapolis *Star Tribune* newspaper. The name of this candidate, his party affiliation or the office for which he was running is not relevant. All candidates of all parties for all offices practice the same rhetoric to varying degrees, some more flagrantly than others, but they all do it. Here is a small part of this speech, that purports to cover issues, as reported in the above newspaper, with the word "fight," used repetitively, underlined (my emphasis).

"I will <u>fight</u> for Americans who know it's not fair when a tax bill costs a trillion dollars and they give 40 percent of it to the richest 1 percent. I will be an advocate for Americans who believe in competitive enterprise but who know the system only works when the books aren't cooked and when the watchdogs have the teeth and budget they need. I will <u>fight</u> for the workers who have seen their pensions melt away and who deserve a Social Security system they can count on. I will <u>fight</u> for the seniors who desperately need prescription drugs under Medicare. I will <u>fight</u> for women who deserve the right to choose. I will <u>fight</u> for the handicapped who deserve lives of dignity, for the mentally ill whose problems aren't theirs alone, but ours. And I will <u>fight</u> as I always have for minorities of all races and religions and sexual orientation who deserve to share in the fullness of American life. I will <u>fight</u> for all people who want to stop this mindless assault on our air, our water and our land and God's beauty. I will <u>fight</u> for citizens who are appalled by the oceans of special interest money that have swamped and compromised the politics of our country."

Whew! That's a lot of fighting!

But what does "fight" really mean, used eight times in this part of the speech? According to one dictionary the number one meaning is "a battle or combat." I interpret that as war. Is that what voters want? I doubt it. If not, why allow it to energize one's self?

Let's analyze other parts of this speech and highlight some key phrases. Who doesn't want "handicapped who deserve lives of dignity," or "minorities of all races and religions and sexual orientation who deserve to share in the fullness of American life?" Is anyone in favor of "workers who have seen their pensions melt away" or "a mindless assault on our air, water and our land and God's beauty?"

Not knowing the speaker's mind, I can only judge the words. In my opinion, this attempt at influencing the voter to believe that candidate is telling them anything, is at the crux of our problem today. What you should be hoping that candidate will tell you, to use just one example, if there has been a "mindless assault on our air, our water and our land," where has this occurred, who is responsible and how, specifically, does the candidate propose to remedy it? Anything less are platitudes and clichés, not meant to explain and instruct, but stimulate and confuse. It's Pablum for the masses.

In this same speech the candidate said, "It is not enough to threaten our enemies with weapons. We must also attract our friends with our values" and, a paragraph later, "We have a United Nations. Let's use it," obviously in justification for this candidates opposition to the United States taking any unilateral military action.

The opposite of "use" is "not use." Have we "not used" the United Nations? Of course not. We have been a member since inception and participated in most of its activities. This sounds appealing, however, to anyone opposed to military action under any circumstances but it ignores the performance of a United Nations with an unparalleled record for ineptness. The number one responsibility of elected leaders of this country is to safeguard the lives and properties of its citizens whether or not they use the auspices of the United Nations to do it. It also ignores the fact this world has changed dramatically in recent decades. Terrorism and nuclear threats from many countries are a factor we never experienced in the early decades of the twentieth century when we could rely on two large oceans to shield us from other parts of the world. We no longer have that luxury, and bold, decisive, preemptive military strikes may be necessary to protect us.

The only cause this candidate overlooked was to "fight for the people who clean our bathrooms" and that category was covered, in those exact words, the preceding evening in a speech by another candidate.

In reality, fighting for the voter or showing independence, is a laugh. The first day the newly elected whomever shows up in the council, legislature, Congress or wherever, the party leader sits him or her down and says, "Listen, buddy, let me tell you how things work around here. If you vote the way we tell you, we'll appoint you to some good committees and maybe you might get a hearing on some bills you'd like to pass to get reelected the next term. If you act independently, we'll put you on a committee to count the deer population, you'll languish in the backroom twiddling your thumbs and no one will ever hear of you or anything you want to do. What'll it be, friend?"

Those so-called promises and all that "fight" talk fly out the window faster than the newly elected whomever can say, "I promise to…"

Why does this happen? Because the voters rarely elect anyone with principles. They elect demagogues and people of weak commitment. The demagogues are easy to spot. It is more difficult to spot the politicians with weak commitment but they can be identified. They're the ones who constantly remind the voters they're "fighting" for them, who promise the voters everything including the sun and the moon, and a few stars thrown in, and the ones who always tell the voter someone else is to blame for their problem. This is usually called playing the race card or the class card or some other card. I call it the jealousy card. That's all it is. Recognize it when you see it. Until the voters make smarter choices, however, we will continue to wallow in our present system. Will it change? Probably not, but it's possible. The reward is a better country for all of us.

The alarming aspect of this problem is the people who attend a political rally and swallow this Pablum, jumping to their feet screaming and yelling whenever they hear the word "fight," are probably the people who actually vote. In the most recent elections less than twenty percent of eligible voters voted in the primaries. In the general elections it was about one-third. It boggles the mind to contemplate the perspective and intelligence, or lack thereof, the other eighty percent, who rarely vote, bring to the serious problems of this country.

Perhaps the most reprehensible part of this sorry mess are the politicians who argue and vote for positions and laws they know are not in the best interests of the citizens but do so only to slow down, embarrass or damage the opposition party. This is evident over and over again. It results from politicians who want to maintain the power of their party forever so they can stay in office forever. They don't look upon their election as a brief opportunity to serve their voters and their country. They view it as a lifetime job and scheme and plan their actions accordingly.

There's an easy solution to this problem. It's called term limits. It's crying out for implementation but voters are not listening. That's why I say, over and over, to all voters, don't blame the politicians for this "sorry mess." Look in the mirror. That's where the blame lies.

A word from history is appropriate here. Frederic Bastiat, famous French economist in the mid-1800s, once wrote, as France was rushing to embrace increasing governmental responsibility in the lives of all their citizens, "The state is the great fiction by which everybody tries to live at the expense of everybody else."

My goodness! What if some history (like Bastiat) was taught in our high schools and colleges? What a profound effect it might have on some young minds as they attempt to apply logic to our problems.

Complicating these problems enormously are a biased media. Platitudes of denial will not change the facts: Ninety percent of the press in recent elections have been voting the same political party. It doesn't matter which party this is. That's a statistic that shows itself through every news or news-entertainment vehicle read or viewed by the American public. It's impossible for the public to be informed of the facts of any event or situation under these circumstances. In fact, they are presently, and will continue to be, grossly misinformed until they demand accurate reporting, interpretation and analysis of the facts.

Other than our educational deficiencies, this problem, in my opinion, is the most serious issue faced by our society today. The bedrock of this country is access to unbiased information. Its absence is stultifying at best, at worst a threat to our survival. The most obvious example is the monopoly newspaper in the majority of cities. You'll remember from my childhood history that we had three newspapers in Minneapolis during the 1930s, all of different persuasions, as did most major cities. Now, most cities have only one daily newspaper. Who's to challenge existing monolithic opinions? No one. They're just thrown out there and allowed to settle. After many years they are embedded so deeply in everyone's psyche they're taken for granted and, worse, assumed to be factual. No country based on the principles of liberty and justice for all can exist for long under these circumstances.

Even as a ten-year-old in the mid-1930s I could recognize bias in the newspaper. I didn't recognize that term, in fact, had probably never heard the word "bias," but it was evident in many reports and articles. As an example, the morning paper might report the details of an ongoing labor strike and emphasize how the strikers were roughed up by the police or how the strikers were unable to feed their families while the strike was in progress and they were short on money. One of the afternoon papers, ideologically different, would emphasize in their report on the strike how the strikers blocked the streets, disrupted traffic and prevented non-union workers, who also desperately needed their pay in those difficult years, from getting to their jobs.

It doesn't take a Rhodes scholar to discern these differences. They're evident if the reader is given TWO papers to read. The problem today is all of us living in cities with only one paper have been desensitized to any opposing viewpoint. We are resigned to accepting the one given us each day and cease to question it. There is also this myth that some newspapers can be neutral, completely impartial, in how they report the news. The only people who are completely neutral have no opinions on anything. That's why they're neutral. Bias is a fact of life for all of us. What's important is to have access to opposing points of view on which to make a decision.

Newspapers have a right to their opinion on the editorial pages. I have no quarrel with that. I do have a quarrel with papers that regularly claim their "neutrality" throughout other sections of the paper. In my opinion, only a competing paper with a differing philosophy can offer balance to the public.

Here is how "neutrality" is regularly disregarded, from my viewpoint. Leaving out the editorial pages where bias is an art form, I find their claim of neutrality disingenuous when ninety percent of all reporters nationwide have been found to vote for candidates of the same political party year after year. One may question this assertion but I believe it has been documented reliably and irrefutably. Given this state of affairs, bias is most obvious in the headlines on the front pages of the newspaper. In articles on which people have a lukewarm interest they may only read the headline but that headline is retained in their consciousness for a long period of time. Headlines at odds, to one degree or another, with the actual story are an everyday occurrence. It's an unparalleled opportunity for the paper's headline editor to inject nuances of his or hers political ideology. This phenomenon occurs whether the piece is reporting a straight news event or a special interest (usually a human interest) article. The choice of stories to appear on the front page is also subject to bias. The reader will assume a story appearing on page one, above the fold, to be more important than on page nineteen, whether that is factual or not, and without realizing some human being at the paper, i.e., an editor about whom they have no knowledge (don't even know their name), made that choice.

Next in line for bias is the choice of all those human interest or "investigative" articles that now make up a substantial portion of the newspaper in most of our large, one-paper cities. In few of these circumstances does the subject matter cry out for publicity. The bulk are chosen by the editor, or whomever supervises the reporters, to influence or buttress other developments where political viewpoints are often paramount. This bias may apply to individuals, to political parties, to government programs, to crimes, almost anything and everything. If the reader, for example, gets a steady diet of problems in agriculture, they're going to slowly but surely believe agriculture is in deep trouble whether the facts support that premise or not. Correspondingly, a constant drumbeat of articles on how the United States is negatively perceived abroad, will lead many readers to come to the conclusion the U.S. is an autocratic dinosaur trampling malevolently over other countries large and small.

In addition to these techniques there are many other opportunities for bias. Opposing facts or opinions may not be in a story until the end (when most readers have abandoned it). Also, questionable (or worse, predictable) sources might be used for "balance" to an article.

Many of these techniques may not even be realized by the people running the paper but constant, unrelenting, singular ideological viewpoints, hidden deep in everyone's soul, color their treatment of a story or event. Consequently, some of these distortions may not be overt in nature but subtle, and their very subtlety, as they are read and digested on a daily basis, fails to alert the reader to their bias or lack of balance.

The bottom line a perceptive reader should ask, when confronted with the possibility of bias, is, "If I was running that paper, would I aggressively attempt to hire reporters with different philosophies from mine or would I prefer reporters and editors of my political and ideological persuasion?" I believe an honest answer would be "No, I'll hire my own kind." And thus you see how easily bias creeps into our newspapers.

So there is the conundrum. What is the answer? At least two newspapers in each city!

Unfortunately, the biggest obstacle to multiple newspapers in large cities is the enormous capital required to start a new paper. The existing paper, assuming there is only one, has a lock on advertising, reporters, news services, even obituaries, a "cash cow," incidentally, at most large papers. For these reasons venture capitalists seem reluctant to fund new papers. I believe this is shortsighted. The risk is no greater than many other start-up businesses but it remains a problem. Few entrepreneurs seem willing to challenge a monopoly press in a large city. Consequently, some alternative capital sources need to be explored. One suggestion is selling stock to the general public. Sports stadiums have been financed by this method. Why not new newspapers which have a great deal more "citizen value." I know I would be willing to buy a fair amount of stock in a second newspaper in my city if only someone with newspaper credentials would knock on my door and ask me. In addition, I would subscribe to it with enthusiasm and glee!

But government intrudes in our lives in numerous other ways, often by passing laws that are illogical, inane and counter-productive to law and order in our society. One example is our current fixation on the evils of racial profiling. Proponents will argue strenuously that it targets specific racial groups. It certainly does and that's exactly why it's necessary. If the police are looking for a suspect of a specific ethnic group in a specific ethnic neighborhood, it's foolish to be restricted from stopping only members of that ethnic group to find the suspect. The pressure to establish quotas that mandate equal percentages of surveillance or deterrence for identifying suspects in law enforcement activities is ridiculous, in fact, without rational justification. The absurdity of this philosophy is apparent with just one example. Police aren't under pressure to stop an equal number of women whenever they are looking for a suspect in a crime or attempting to prevent crime. Why not? Women make up about fifty percent of our population. How can police prejudge that women are not good suspects in street crime, drug running, gang shooting or whatever? It's easy. History tells us they are not.

Attempts to make it appear we are not profiling members of the ethnic group that are responsible for destruction of the World Trade Center, and similar recent terrorist attacks, is equally ridiculous. It's more than ridiculous, however. It's compromising the safety of our country. On each occasion that we spend time and money investigating people of all ethnic groups for crimes clearly associated with a specific ethnic group, we are placing the lives of all our citizens in needless jeopardy.

Apropos of many subjects in this book and particularly this chapter on government, I quote frequently from the digest *Imprimis*, reprinted by permission from *Imprimis*, the national speech digest of Hillsdale College, Hillsdale, Michigan (www.hillsdale.edu). In the November, 2002 edition, they printed a speech by their president, Larry P. Arnn, delivered earlier at a conference, that pinpoints many of the changes in our lives in recent decades that mirror changes in the government. He states, in reference to the philosophy of his college and changes in our country, "In the 30 years since *Imprimis* was founded, the U.S. economy has grown in real terms two-and-one-half times, while the federal government has grown eight times." He continues, "let us look at America. Right now it is engaged in a great battle. It is not only the obvious and urgent battle with terrorism, but also a battle over the meaning of the country itself."

Founded in 1844, Hillsdale, a small college, accepts no federal student aid money. Mr. Arnn continues, "if young people go to college with the understanding that they have a right to go, and therefore that someone else is obliged to pay for it, they learn a lesson about the meaning of rights. If they go to a college where their scholarships and loans are provided by private citizens, who give their money voluntarily...they learn something else." He finished the speech with, "The history of Hillsdale College is in fact nothing other or less than the telling, on a smaller scale, of the history of our nation. Because we (the College) have held fast to the faith of our original creed, we have been in conflict now for a long time with the government that we have also fought bravely, at every time of need, to preserve. We are not given other tools than study and learning, prayer and devotion, argument and action, with which to defend our liberty. If a little College (like Hillsdale) can stand for that through war and trial, anyone can do it." We would be well to step back and examine issues like this more carefully. Governmental (and corporate) malfeasance abounds. We are too young as a nation to be making these monumental errors. Somehow we muddle along but muddling won't work forever.

Are there lessons to be learned from the Great Depression days? Yes, there are. Remedies in transportation, taxation, voting practices, governmental efficiency, common sense in racial profiling and media bias all cry out for solutions. They weren't as obviously flawed in the 1930s. Does that trouble you? It should!

♦Chapter Nine: **SAFETY**

Here again, I state in advance, is a contrast highly in favor of the depression years of the 1930s.

I lived in a middle-class neighborhood in Minneapolis not unlike thousands of other neighborhoods in this country. There was a large Sears Roebuck retail store two blocks from our house. I rode my bike there at least once a week, left it parked outside the store, unlocked, and it was never stolen. In fact, I never owned a lock for my bike in all the years I used it.

On Thursdays I rode my bike downtown to get a copy of the *Sporting News* newspaper. In those days the paper was a baseball-only weekly that carried information, scores and league standings on all the four hundred plus teams in organized professional baseball. It came in by railroad from wherever it was published about ten o'clock in the morning. I was there waiting for it when the newsstand operator cut the string on the bundle and placed copies for sale on the display rack. In all those trips downtown and to other places in the city I was never once harassed, molested or in any way bothered by strangers. In fact, my mother never warned me to "Watch out for strangers." It simply wasn't a problem. Molestation, improper advances from strangers, pedophilia, was not a topic of conversation in our household. It wasn't necessary!

Contrast this with the statement I heard on television on November 26, 2002, by a superintendent of schools in a local suburb of Minneapolis, in response to sightings of two suspicious men near schools trying to entice young boys into cars. He said, and I must paraphrase it, "We teach safety precautions (from predators) to our students on an equal basis with reading and arithmetic." No doubt this is correct and no doubt he was proud of this achievement.

Which do you prefer for personal safety? The 1930s or the 2000s? It's an easy choice, a no-brainer, as they say.

There was a neighborhood movie theater two blocks from our house. My stepmother's daughter and her female friends frequently walked to this theater and back home again around ten to eleven o'clock in the evening. Occasionally this daughter walked to and from the theater by herself and met her friends there. Again, not once were these women attacked, molested or even suffered improper advances that I can remember.

Once in the theater they settled back comfortably and enjoyed the movie without distractions from people in adjacent seats eating and drinking as if in a restaurant. They also weren't distracted by security people, prevalent today, patrolling every fifteen minutes to squelch rowdy behavior.

Contrast this, for example, with the conditions prevalent today for the safety of women in Minneapolis and probably every other large city in the United States. On February 21, 2003, the Minneapolis *Star Tribune* reported on a robber and rapist the police were trying to apprehend, suspected of half-a-dozen or more assaults in a six-week period. The article ended with the information that the police department "hopes to set up a free personal-safety workshop (for women) in the next few weeks." It then listed the following *tips* from the Minneapolis Police Department, "after a series of attempted kidnappings and sexual assaults...to reduce your risk": Try to be escorted by someone you trust or a member of your company's security staff; Look inside your car before you get inside; Lock your doors as soon as you get inside your car. Keep your windows up, even while driving; Don't pull over or unlock your door to offer help to someone. Instead, use your cell phone to call for help for the person; Watch for people you don't know loitering in parking lots and vehicles; Walk and park on well-lighted, busy streets; Carry a noise-making device, such as a whistle or screech alarm; yell or honk your car's horn to call attention to your situation; Go directly to an area where there are other people if you feel uneasy.

Again, I could just about answer my question, posed in the introduction to this book, "Which (world) do you want for your future, the 1930s or the 2000s?" It's really tragic we make all these technological advances in our society and allow the personal side of our lives to deteriorate to these levels.

An older woman whom I read about last year said she had never heard the term "date rape" until she read stories about it in the newspaper recently. "Apparently our suitors had more respect for us in those days," she was reported to have said.

Contrast this with the paranoia that exists today. Women in any neighborhood don't dare walk the streets unescorted in the evening and in some neighborhoods at no time of day. Mothers are continually warning their young children to watch out for strangers and not to speak to anyone they do not know at any time. Pedophiles aren't confined to schools or churches. They roam all over the country and are a constant threat to young children. Muggings and robberies are so commonplace in most cities they are never listed or mentioned in daily newspapers except at the end of the year when the local politicians publish some statistics trying to convince the voters crime is down and their city is a bastion of safety. Four or five years ago Minneapolis gained the name Murderapolis because they were one hundred murders in that single year. This is in a city with a population of less than half a million people. I'm certain some larger cities eclipsed that dubious record and continue to suffer under those appalling conditions.

In addition to date rape another new term to enter our lexicon in the past decade or two is road rage. What's the answer, the experts suggest? Look the other way. Don't make eye contact. That's how we train people encountering dogs. Don't make eye contact! The dog will feel threatened. How much further will we go in "blaming the victim" before we wake up and say "Enough is enough. I want to take back my world!"

Defenders of the status quo will say, "The current decade is no worse than the 1930s. Newspapers and television just report more of it now and people hear it more quickly and more loudly." There's a bit of truth to that but only a small bit. Remember, in 1930, every major city had multiple newspapers, some emphasizing sensational news to sell papers. Everyone had a radio to which they were glued at news hour and the cities geographically were much smaller where news could travel from neighborhood to neighborhood rapidly. If someone on the block was harmed, everyone on the block had heard the news two hours later. No, the culprit is not the media. It's us! And there aren't any easy solutions. Tough problems usually require tough solutions, unfortunately.

There are cities today, at the beginning of the twenty-first century, where violent gangs have taken over portions of the city. We all know the identity of these locations. It's easy to blame the police for not cleaning these up and they may share in the blame. However, I believe the police are tired of watching judges give these violent offenders light sentences or probation where it is unwarranted, they are tired of watching residents turn their back on criminal activities, they are tired of attorneys, who know these violent criminals are guilty, using every technicality and trick in the book to get them off, they are tired of juries sympathetic to environment as an excuse for crime and, most of all, tired of a "blame the cops first" attitude from significant segments of the population.

If all those problems aren't sufficient to exacerbate the gang-related problem, now law enforcement has to deal with the threat of terrorism. No one will identify how many enforcement personnel at all levels have been transferred to terrorism details but it must be a monumental number. There have been reports in daily newspapers that gang-related activities have been rising as law enforcement resources have been reassigned.

All of this makes it easy for society as a whole to turn its back on supporting the job of cleaning up bad neighborhoods but if we don't have the stomach to clean up our own mess, who will?

This same situation exists today in world affairs. The United States is now the preeminent world power. If we don't take the initiative in solving world problems, who will? Not the other nations who are jealous and envious of our power and position. And certainly not the United Nations over half of whom do not have freely elected governments and a substantial number with tyrannies that routinely practice unspeakable human rights violations on their own people. It is probably not an exaggeration to say that the United Nations is a first class world employment agency with vested conflicts among member countries so severe and pervasive it will never be able to deal forcefully with any world problem.

But safety has many dimensions. Is our food supply safer now? I doubt it. For all the oversight we are supposed to have from government regulation there seems to be a never-ending stream of food poisoning cases and similar problems in the restaurant and food supply industry. The effects of food poisoning don't always end with a bad case of diarrhea. There can be permanent kidney damage, reactive arthritis (inflammation of the joints) that can last a lifetime, gallbladder disease and damage to the stomach lining. It can be especially damaging to children.

A primary cause may be the mechanization and production line environment of the animals used for food. In the 1930s farmers brought their eggs and chickens to town where they were distributed by wholesalers to the retail grocer. These were chickens running around a barnyard somewhere eating grasshoppers (which were plentiful in those days), small nails and other assorted debris that chickens eat. In the process they received a varied diet that protected them against the hazards of eating the same feed day after day, month after month. Today these chickens spend their entire life in a cage so small they can barely turn around and may feed on ground up chicken parts procured as a byproduct of their own slaughtering process. Added to this eclectic mix is a potpourri of chemicals spread on agricultural crops whose effect on humans no one can measure, especially long-term.

The amount of these chemicals, herbicides, pesticides and other 'cides dumped on field crops is a calamity waiting to be exposed. Periodically a report or study pops up claiming a higher rate of birth defects and/or cancer among farmers using large amounts of pesticides. If these studies have relevance for farmers just working with crops, not ingesting them, think what danger this portends for consumers eating products from these crops. The antibiotics given to all animals used for food or the production of food is equally alarming. And every time some studies on these dangers gain some publicity the chemical companies rush to squash them.

My family will not drink milk from cows treated with synthetic bovine growth hormone. This is a hormone designed to increase milk production in cows. The Food and Drug Administration (FDA) approves the use of the hormone. Despite this approval, because of studies that have suggested a link between this hormone and increased infections in cows, some people have made the choice to not drink milk from cows treated with this hormone.

Tremendous pressure on legislators, however, has prevented farmers and food processors, who do not give this hormone to their cows, from labeling milk or other dairy products with statements they are free of this growth hormone. Instead, the milk we drink has a statement on the carton that reads, "Milk from cows not treated with rBST [the chemical name for the hormone]. No significant difference has been shown between milk derived from rBST treated and non-rBST treated cows." In all innocence, then, I might ask, "Why are so many people switching to milk free of this growth hormone?" The display space for this milk in the local supermarket has increased each year. A growing number of people are obviously not reassured by FDA pronouncements. It's no wonder one of the fastest growing trends in the country is organic foods. The general population is awakening, however slowly, to many of these dangers.

But eternal vigilance is the price for even organic farming which is the practice of growing foodstuffs without synthetic fertilizers or pesticides. Congress recently passed legislation that allowed conventional (non-organic feed) to be given to animals, and the feed labeled as organic, if the organic feed cost twice as much. The provision, as is common, slipped through by being attached to a larger bill unrelated to farming. These deceitful practices for achieving the objectives of special interests are common in Congress.

Fortunately, this provision, detrimental to the intent and the purpose for labeling products organic, was quickly discovered and an attempt will be mounted to repeal that provision. However, a repeal is not a slam-dunk and, while that is underway, hopefully with success, the label "organic" doesn't really insure organic products for that segment of the food industry.

I don't remember in my childhood of any talk, must less experience, with a food product we purchased from the grocery store or meat market that was found to be harmful. I'm sure there must have been some but that was not a routine event as it is today. Amazingly, all of this was at a period when our only refrigeration in the home was from an icebox, cooled by a chunk of ice delivered daily by an iceman, or every other day, depending on the size of one's icebox. Mechanization and automation have their advantages but also their perils and it is showing up today in many products in this so-called advanced society. In addition to all this we now have mad cow disease, SARS (severe acute respiratory syndrome) and West Nile virus to name just a few of our current plagues.

Another difference is our exposure to the millions of illegal immigrants in this country. If you're an illegal immigrant, you've broken the law. That doesn't speak well for one's respect for this country. It also increases the probability that person will break the law again.

Undoubtedly there were some illegal immigrants in this country in the 1930s but I believe the problem today is one hundred if not one thousand times more severe. How many of today's illegals are terrorists waiting to spread destruction? We don't know but that is exactly the problem: We don't know. I don't remember terrorism or even the remote possibility of terrorism as a problem in the 1930s. Now, in the first decade of the twenty-first century, screening and detention at our borders and issuance of visas is a joke, even in the wake of the destruction of the World Trade Centers in 2001.

And terrorism is not the only crime illegal immigrants may commit. Plain old nuisance crime like social security and credit card forgery, petty theft, passing bad checks, auto theft, driving without a license or a forged license, and on and on, ad infinitum. The Immigration and Naturalization Service (INS), in some areas, apparently, routinely ignores violators of these crimes when local police arrest them and report their illegal status. As a result they are often given light sentences by sympathetic judges, or released on low bail prior to any sentencing, and promptly disappear until their next arrest.

Meanwhile taxpayers in this country are forced to pay the bills for added police protection, fraudulent welfare claims, jails to house them in the rare cases they are retained, and the dangers inherent in the crimes they commit while they are roaming the country unknown, undocumented and unaccounted for in any registration process.

When the INS does decide to initiate deportation proceedings against some illegal immigrants, their advocates and activists file lawsuits to prevent it and judges routinely grant injunctions or restraining orders tying up the deportations for months or years or forever. An Associated Press story on November 29, 2002, reported a typical (my word, not theirs) example where INS wanted to deport three illegal immigrants from a third world country who had already been convicted in this country of "drug, drunken driving or assault charges." The rationale for denying this deportation was "(country) has no functioning government that could agree to accept deportees." In other words, given half the countries in this world have "no functioning government" or governments that torture, suppress or mistreat their people in one way or the other, the United States, apparently, is responsible for the care and support of all those people. With a world population of six billion, that translates into three billion people that could or should find sanctuary in this country and we had better find some way to add them to our two hundred and eighty million citizens. What idiocy! I don't know how this country can survive these types of rationalizations.

Are all illegal immigrants breaking our laws (in addition to the law they broke in entering the country)? Of course not. The majority are probably otherwise law-abiding residents, if not citizens. However, with our illegal immigrant population now estimated at twelve million, if only one percent of these illegals are pursuing criminal activities, that's one hundred and twenty thousand people roaming around with no record of who they are, their past offenses, where they come from, where they live or any history whatsoever. In all likelihood the percentage engaged in illegal activities of some type is far greater than one percent suggesting multiple hundreds of thousands are loose in this country to pursue illegal activities after illegal entry.

It would be easy to fill the next one hundred pages with excerpts from numerous books published recently on the subject of border control – or lack of it – but anyone genuinely concerned about this problem has probably read some of them. If you doubt this is a major problem, I implore you to read *Invasion*, by Michelle Malkin, published in 2002 by Regnery Publishing, Inc. This book is three hundred and thirty-two pages of the most chilling, frightening, almost unbelievable, account of the deplorable state of security and lack of protection from the government departments and organizations currently responsible for enforcing our immigration laws. I believe, today, this is our most serious law enforcement problem. Citizens of the United States have the right to expect their government to protect them from non-citizens entering this country illegally, some with the prime objective of breaking its laws and/or fomenting terrorism. Wars with other nations are an infrequent occurrence. Violence from alien criminals, roaming freely among us, is perpetrated every day. Please! Read *Invasion*, price $27.95 from your local bookstore.

My ancestors waited years to immigrate to this country. Men came over alone because the immigration quota for their country was insufficient to allow their wife or children to come with them. The point is made that this immigration, primarily from Europe, has enriched our society, so, therefore, in an astonishing leap of logic, all immigration, no matter how haphazardly contrived or controlled, must be beneficial for this country.

Yes, European immigration did enrich our society but it was a controlled immigration in accordance with established quotas. In the Great Depression years of the early 1930s, legal immigration was between twenty thousand to thirty-five thousand per year. Today legal immigration is almost one million per year. A substantial number are granted citizenship on a hodgepodge of visas created to fit all classifications of people wishing to immigrate. Illegal immigration is estimated to be an additional half-million per year with the aforementioned total of twelve million or more illegal immigrants now in this country. It is uncontrolled, chaotic and can only be damaging to us in the long run.

Population estimates forecast the descendants of white Europeans will be a minority in this country in a period somewhere around fifty years or less. Figures from *World Population Prospects, The 2000 Revision*, by the Population Division, Department of Economic and Social Affairs, of the United Nations Secretariat, show the **more developed regions** of the world, with an estimated population in the year 2000 of 1,191,000,000, are expected to grow to only 1,309,000,000, or **ten percent**, in the year 2050. The estimates for the populations of the **less developed regions** are 4,865,000,000 in 2000 and growth to 8,141,000,000, or **sixty-seven percent,** in 2050. By region the estimates are (for the years 2000 and 2050, in millions), Africa 794 to 2000, Asia 3,672 to 5,428, Europe 727 to 603, Latin America & Caribbean 519 to 806, North America (including the United States) 314 to 436 and Oceana 31 to 47.

The report adds, "The difference in growth trajectories between the more developed and the less developed regions is mainly the product of their current levels of fertility and the path fertility is expected to follow in the future. Although considerable differences in fertility exist among the countries of the more developed regions, in virtually all of them fertility is currently below replacement level (i.e. below 2.1 children per woman).

As the immigration to the United States is currently from the less developed countries, particularly illegal immigration, our population increases can safely be forecasted to duplicate the population increases of those countries. These statistics have a double significance. With a sixty-seven percent growth rate forecasted in the less developed countries by 2050, the pressure for their people to immigrate to the United States will only increase. Once in the U.S., legally or illegally, their numbers will likely grow at the same sixty-seven percent rate! If we continue to accept one million legal immigrants each year, a half-million illegal immigrants (plus the twelve million illegal already here), and all these immigrants have a sixty-seven percent growth rate, I won't even estimate for you the total immigrants in the United States by the year 2050. You're welcome to do the arithmetic!

No nation has survived long as a melting pot of these proportions and diversity. We will soon be a nation of nations. An assortment of people from all over the world will not assimilate cohesively as a nation, respecting its rights, ready to defend and die for all others in the country in times of crisis. A nation needs a core constituency that honors the principles and ideals on which that nation was founded. This unity of purposeful allegiance is essential for stability. This is particularly relevant if each group of immigrants demands full acceptance of all their native customs and language and exhibits hostility to the principles and foundations on which this country began.

The United States might successfully assimilate up to one million LEGAL immigrants per year if all ethnic groups show some

143

reasonable forbearance to our customs and traditions. Uncontrolled, chaotic, mixing of millions more ILLEGAL immigrants from diverse ethnic groups will not successfully assimilate. This isn't prejudice. It's common sense.

All political parties in this country are guilty of failure to confront this problem and we all share the blame. It's one of those problems that gets lost in concern for the economy, employment or other rationalizations and we look the other way while it grows to unmanageable proportions. We collectively wake up one morning and there is no solution short of violence. Is that too strong a prognostication? I think not. Illegal immigration and all the problems it portends for the near future may be the most serious, unresolved domestic issue today in this country as it impacts safety for all citizens.

But there are others in addition to those already enumerated. The justice system is moving ever closer to protecting criminals at the expense of victims. This is a prime safety issue that has grown largely unnoticed since the 1930s. There is an increasing reluctance to hold criminals responsible. Instead every excuse is offered to reduce their responsibility and blame the victim for some portion of the crime or, worst of all, blame "society."

The most flagrant example is the rush to excoriate the police whenever they use force to halt criminal activities.Yes, a small minority of police are brutal or falsify evidence or fail to do their job but the vast majority are brave and honest and the only protection between law-abiding citizens and anarchy in this country. If you doubt that statement, visualize what would happen to us if we disbanded the police forces today and told everyone they were on their own? I know what I would do: Get a gun and prepare to defend my home from invaders.

Given this scenario we should be idolizing our law enforcement personnel and backing their life threatening occupation without reservation. To constantly denigrate and question every action of the "cops" is ludicrous and insane for a society that professes respect for the sanctity of laws and the safety of citizens.

The present legal system bears a major responsibility for this attitude. Their motto is "sue, sue, sue and sue again" and don't leave any reputation or target unblemished if there is a dollar to be squeezed out of it. The outrageous, misleading accusations a significant portion of attorneys throw around carelessly is repugnant and appalling. All this accomplishes, other than enriching some claimants, is to make average citizens afraid to pursue or speak out against corruption in society for fear of being sued. This is pathetic and the problem is becoming worse by the day.

So many juries are handing down verdicts for such large sums against doctors and hospitals that doctors can no longer afford malpractice insurance and must either move to states more sympathetic to doctors or cease practice. A doctor shortage in this country is imminent and, simultaneously, we need more doctors, not fewer. Concurrently, juries are giving damages for BILLIONS (not millions) to a person with lung cancer who has been warned repeatedly not to smoke and more millions to someone whose coffee was too hot when they spilled it on themselves at a fast-food restaurant. Come on! Where is reality?

In the next breath we're told identify theft (stealing credit card numbers, bank account numbers, etc.) and mail-tampering is a national crisis. This is followed by news that in the year 2002 the State of California has lost track of 33,000 convicted sex offenders or forty-four percent of the 76,000 sex offenders registered with the State. To add insult to injury, no one in the California State Justice Department, which apparently "oversees" all this, can estimate the cost of the present program, much less the danger to public safety of 33,000 untracked sex offenders.

None of these facts in the year 2002 seem to disturb the public's aplomb regarding safety, however. To illustrate, there are in excess of six hundred traffic fatalities a year in the State of Minnesota. If four airliners crashed in one year in this State, each with one hundred and fifty people on board, the airlines headquartered here would either be grounded or doing double and triple inspections on every plane before takeoff. If terrorists blew up our largest office building in downtown Minneapolis with a loss of life of six hundred people, the number of citizens in Minnesota marching and demonstrating against war would plummet as they received news of the loss of their friends and relatives.

What is real and what is fantasy? Hypocrisy? A lot! Common sense? Very little!

As an aside, of no particular relevance, I suppose, asbestos-cement pipes were a big item in World War II, trumpeted for their shock resistance, light weight and resistance to corrosion. I guess we had our blind spots in those days also.

Yet another concern today is our reluctance to protect our citizens visiting or living in foreign countries. Too often the decisions of who to protect are based on our political relationship with the foreign country, not the welfare or lives of our citizens. As I write this in the year 2003 there have been egregious examples of some of our embassies turning away United States citizens who go up to the gates of the foreign embassy pleading to enter. If they persist, Marine Corp. guards will forcibly push them away.

This is indefensible in a country based on protecting its citizens. If that trend continues, we may as well remove our embassies from these countries and reduce the risk of terrorism to which they are continually exposed. This also sends a signal to countries unsympathetic to our national interests that the United States is weak and unwilling to protect or fight for its interests.

Sadly, we have not learned this lesson in the last seventy years. The United States watched while Adolf Hitler and Germany stomped all over Europe in the 1930s and Japan terrorized and murdered populations in countries all over Asia. A good example of this is the sinking of the United States gunboat Panay in 1937. On patrol in the Yangtze River in China to protect American citizens in China's civil war, it came under attack near Nanking from Japanese forces rampaging through China raping and killing Chinese in unprecedented numbers. Read *The Rape of Nanking* by Iris Chang, published in 1997 by Basic Books, a Subsidiary of Perseus Books, L.L.C., if you have any doubts about that history.

The Panay was sunk in December, 1937 with heavy loss of life by militant Japanese forces anxious to draw the United States into a war with them. The temporary furor over this incident quickly subsided when other factions of the Japanese government, apparently not ready to attack the United States just yet, said it was all a mistake and apologized to us. The American people, very much isolationist at that time, gladly accepted this explanation and returned to solving their economic concerns. The folly of this was evident four years later at Pearl Harbor.

History is supposed to teach us lessons. The lessons are there; we just fail to learn them.

But the increasing danger to the United States from our enemies abroad surely exceeds all other dangers. In World Wars I and II, and subsequent wars, we were opposed by one nation or a coalition of nations. Our targets were located in specific geographical areas. Today our enemy is scattered throughout the world, a shadowy, mobile, ill-defined alliance of individuals and part-nations difficult and oftentimes impossible to identify or locate.

We should assume these enemies have biological, chemical and, shortly, nuclear weapons of mass murder. Biological weapons are probably the greatest threat. A smallpox epidemic can damage this country more quickly than a nuclear attack. The reason is the relative ease with which smallpox can be spread simultaneously in many areas and the time it takes for a population to protect itself by vaccination especially when a large segment of the population has already taken the stance that vaccination is not urgent. Biological capabilities and threats are also transportable by multiple individuals to multiple locations and difficult to uncover or identify in advance. Nuclear delivery systems, on the other hand, are intricate, cumbersome and usually identifiable in advance. It would be difficult for our enemies to mount more than one or two nuclear strikes before this nation responded with counter-strikes obliterating that enemy.

If the threat of a smallpox epidemic is insufficient to strike terror in your heart and soul, I heard recently on a late-night radio broadcast that terrorists are working on combining smallpox with the Ebola virus. The combination would be a disease so virulent, so deadly the implications are unimaginable. And don't laugh about what one might hear on late-night radio. If you believe our government, this year or any year, tells us all the possibilities we face for annihilation, you are sadly mistaken.

This country has never been in the vulnerable position it is today. The reason is the advance of technology. We may have the largest concentration of technologically advanced weapons but that proliferation has also given our enemies the capability for weapons they never were able to acquire in a less-advanced world. The other difference is we will use our capabilities for peaceful or defensive purposes. Our enemies will use their capabilities, reduced they may be, for attacks without provocation, warning or moral consequences. People, or nations, adhering to religious or moral principles are always at a disadvantage in this type of conflict. We should also have no doubts that the weapons arrayed against us are prevalent in more than one clandestine society currently plotting our destruction. Russia had substantial quantities of all of these. The subsequent fragmentation of that country, which took place in the past decade, left thousands of their weapons scientists to search for new "homes" for their services. A majority undoubtedly found eager recipients and the "nuclear club" is growing.

This world, our wonderful country, has changed and I fear too few of us realize it. I remember in the 1980s when I worked for a national association headquartered in New York, I traveled extensively on the East Coast and throughout the country on their behalf. I could run to catch a shuttle at LaGuardia airport with only a comely flight attendant holding the tramway door for me and saying, "Hurry, Sir. We're about to depart. You're the last one to board," and paying for the ticket after we were airborne. I also remember running from one end of O'Hare to the other to make a connection at the last minute, unimpeded by any scrutiny, to board an earlier flight on which I was not booked but had seats available, and would get me to my destination hours in advance of my ticketed schedule.

As I settled back comfortably in my seat, and the plane rose swiftly into the clouds and then above them into bright sunshine, I didn't glance around furtively to see who might be exhibiting terrorist tendencies. The other passengers seemed content to be aboard and alone with their thoughts. I probably dug a book out of my briefcase for some uninterrupted reading time. In the 1980s I was enthralled with the exploits of Beryl Markham, the first person to fly the Atlantic solo, against the headwinds, from England to North America, in 1936. I read everything about her I could find, especially her memoir *West with the Night*, detailing her life in Africa, first published in 1942 and re-released in 1987 by North Point Press, an engrossing, riveting book about a life, a culture, we have lost forever. An endorsement by Ernest Hemingway to *West with the Night,* said, in part, "I knew her fairly well in Africa and never would have suspected that she could and would put pen to paper except to write in her flyer's log book. As it is, she has written so well, and marvelously well, that I was completely ashamed of myself as a writer. I felt that I was simply a carpenter with words, picking up whatever was furnished on the job and nailing them together and sometimes making an okay pig pen. But [she] can write rings around all of us who consider ourselves as writers."

High praise from a master!

I digress here only to show you the contentment associated with traveling and flying in the 1980s. Contrast that with the anxiety we experience traveling and flying today. Will it ever return to those idyllic days? I fear not! Now we face a gauntlet to board an airplane with restrictions at every step. This is not the same country it was only a decade or two ago. How has it deteriorated so rapidly? Because we assumed good times were perpetual and no defense or sacrifice was necessary to maintain them. Large segments of the population today are still asleep. In a perverse way an example of this malaise is what happened during the 2002 Thanksgiving holiday. Sixteen thousand airline passengers tried to board planes with pocket knives in their possession. Where have these people been since the World Trade Centers were demolished? On the moon? Don't they ever read a newspaper or even listen to the nightly news explaining knives are not allowed? I doubt there was a terrorist among them. These are just people representative of too large a segment of society who haven't the foggiest notion – and don't care – about what is going on in the world or even the country in which they live and breathe.

This current precarious state of affairs is why we need to elevate the global threats against us to priority number one in this country and find some solution for the other threats, namely to control legal immigration and the sloppy issuance of visas, to STOP illegal immigration, to reduce crime, particularly crime associated with pedophilia, reduce pesticides dumped on our food supply and cease excoriating our police whenever they must use force to maintain the law. These problems did not exist in the 1930s. That is the lesson we can learn today. Safety of our citizens whether from enemies abroad or enemies within should be priority number one for a country's government.

Are there lessons to be learned from the Great Depression days? Yes, there are. The people in this country need to begin spending more of their time pondering the level of their security and less on their 401K. A well-known radio commentator frequently makes the statement, "Ten percent of the people pull the cart in this country. The other ninety percent ride in it." That's disastrous for the long-term welfare of a democracy. There's a country at stake here, not just a new house and a vacation in Acapulco.

♦Chapter Ten: **PATRIOTISM**

Oh, my! Once again the contrast here is striking. We continue to debate and haggle over whether students should recite the Pledge of Allegiance in school and whether flag burning is an acceptable practice.

Suffice to say these were not questions in the 1930s. Students were pleased to recite the Pledge and burning the flag would have been cause for mayhem wherever it was done. That these are now questions hotly debated is the best imprimatur of a society in patriotic decline. I grew up reciting this Pledge and probably remember the words more easily than the Star Spangled Banner, the Lord's Prayer or any similar recitations: *I pledge allegiance to the flag of the United States of America and to the Republic for which it stands, one nation, under God, indivisible, with liberty and justice for all.*

And that's considered objectionable and blasphemous by its opponents!

The primary objection, among others, is to the words, "under God." This nation was founded on religious principles, to escape religious tyranny. The first amendment to the Constitution, previously referenced in this book, warrants repeating. It says, "Congress shall make no law respecting an establishment of religion, or **prohibiting the free exercise thereof**; or abridging the freedom of speech, or of the press, or the right of the people peaceably to assemble, and to petition the Government for a redress of grievances." That we should eradicate any reference to God in our patriotic pledges is contrary to the principles of our foundation. It's also illogical.

Is the Star Spangled Banner next to be banned because it includes a reference to God? Most of us know the first verse but few know there are four verses. These were inspired when Francis Scott Key saw the American flag still flying after a night of bombardment of an American fort by the British navy in the War of 1812, a war declared by the United States to stop Britain from numerous violations of our sovereignty. This is the fourth verse, the only one with a reference to God in it, but a verse almost equal in patriotic power to the first one.

> Oh! Thus be it ever, when freemen shall stand
> Between their loved homes and the war's desolation!
> Blest with victory and peace, may the heaven-rescued land
> Praise the Power that hath made and preserved us a nation.
> Then conquer we must, for our cause it is just,
> And this be our motto: "In God is our trust."
> And the star-spangled banner in triumph shall wave
> O'er the land of the free and the home of the brave.

This objection to God comes from many sources but supporters of atheism are the most vocal. If this country were founded on the principles of atheism, would they object to any reference to atheism in their constitution or national pledges? Of course not. Tolerance for one's viewpoint is easy when it agrees with your own, but more difficult when there is disagreement.

One can only detect in many of these problems a turn away from patriotism and a concerted effort to obscure truth and confidence in one's country.

I don't cover religion as a separate topic in this book primarily because, unfortunately, the mere mention of it inflames so many people and renders dialogue on any topic useless. In fact, I authored a book recently, a novel, where it was logical to include in the title the word "church" and additional references to religion in the promotion of the book. I was advised on several occasions to delete such references. Any deviation from strictly secular connotations is frowned upon by the majority of the publishing establishment in the belief it alienates people.

Churches may even appear to be moving in this direction. A forty-eight million dollar church with a 4500 seat sanctuary was built recently in Minnesota and purposely designed to "be mistaken for a corporate headquarters or education institution," according to an article in the August 20, 2002, Minneapolis *Star Tribune* newspaper. Non-denominational, of course, its pastor is quoted as saying, "We want to be welcoming to people who might not consider themselves religious," and, the article continues, might avoid a building that looked like a traditional church.

My first reaction to this was to question if this degree of secularization was in accord with the original intent of a church? I couldn't fault the pastor. He was only trying to attract members to teach them the Gospel by whatever means necessary. Then I found out more about this church. I found it was a church devoted to helping people, devoted to teaching them all the lessons to be learned from the Bible, devoted to making their religious experience enrich their lives and the lives of all with whom they came in contact.

The moral here, and I use the word unpretentiously, is don't allow your actions to be determined by what is perceived to be popular opinion. I wish I had the opportunity to re-title my novel. I mistakenly allowed a segment of "popular opinion" to influence me out of proportion to what I should have known to be relevant.

Notwithstanding all of the above, a recent ministerial transplant to Minnesota from Norway, who had accepted the call to be the pastor of a local Minneapolis church, was reported in an article in the Minneapolis *Star Tribune* newspaper on October 6, 2002, saying, "only three percent of the population (of Norway) attend church services." This, despite the fact, "The Lutheran Church in Norway is a state church, and the government pays the pastor's salary and takes care of the church." He continued, "Here (in America), I get to know people before they die." The moral: Learn the facts before you make a judgment. I had always assumed church attendance was high in Norway.

Another subject, I must decry, never countenanced in the 1930s, is flag burning which is, at its basic, a reprehensible practice, a contemptuous affront to every citizen who values their citizenship.

It's a particular insult to the millions of service people who have given their bodies and their lives in defense of this country of which the Stars and Stripes are a symbol. It is unlikely any of these flag burners would give anything in their possession, much less their legs or arms or eyes or lives, for this country. Flag burning isn't "free speech." It's free anarchy. Is that what we want for the future of the United States?

Akin to flag burning are street protests against war when the country is *in a war*! It is an insult to the thousands of wives, husbands, sons, daughters, aunts, uncles and grandparents of all the men and women in the armed forces. These relatives are praying each day for the end to hostilities and a safe return of their loved one. They don't need protestors denouncing the war and suggesting it's an immoral, irrelevant, scurrilous adventure perpetrated by a warmongering government. This is a slap in the face to the military personnel placing their life in jeopardy so the balance of us can live in freedom.

The chant "We support our troops" (but oppose the war) is equally indefensible. It's a ridiculous, monumental cop-out. It's impossible to support the troops unless one hopes they will defeat the enemy – and that's about the last desire of the majority of protestors. One should ask oneself why peace protestors are so insensitive as to demonstrate against a conflict already in progress? The answer may surprise you. It isn't a protest against war. Like most protests, regardless of the stated purpose, these are protests of political ideologies. The war (or whatever the announced reason) is a convenient excuse to make a political statement and/or push the protestor's political ideology. In the case of recent war protests the result was even more insidious. The protestors tied up local law enforcement people who should have been available for guarding the country against terrorist attacks.

But lately even a war is not required for mobs to take over the streets. The cause celebre for recent student demonstrations is winning an athletic championship. Thousands of students demonstrated in 2002 after the University of Minnesota hockey team won an NCAA (National Collegiate Athletic Association) championship. The team won again in 2003 and this time a "near-riot" (local police terminology) ensued. I would term 2,000 students torching five vehicles, setting one hundred fires, tearing down traffic signals, and various other acts of mayhem and maliciousness lasting for several hours, and requiring almost 150 police from four different agencies to quell, a full blown riot. However, we mustn't offend the tender sensibilities of these young students so eager to learn (something), albeit it the fine art of rioting. The University president was quoted, in connection with the riots, as "beyond just being upset!"

Who will pay for these youthful "indiscretions"? One guess: the taxpayers!

Webster's Encyclopedic Unabridged Dictionary defines patriotism as "a devoted love, support, and defense of one's country; national loyalty." That should not be too much to expect of a citizen, in a time of conflict, who lives in the country, enjoys all its bounty, raises and educates his children here and accepts the protection of its laws.

As a veteran of World War II, I find flag burning and thoughtless protests particularly onerous. My service was undistinguished from millions of other service personnel and I would admit that when I enlisted (was not drafted) in the U.S. Navy at the age of seventeen in December, 1941, immediately after Pearl Harbor, patriotism was not the first consideration on my mind. All my friends were going, my high school offered to give me my diploma several weeks early (we had mid-school-year graduation in those days) and the thrill of the moment for a teenager was probably paramount in my mind.

Nevertheless, I was in service until March of 1946 and, along with some admittedly cushy assignments in the States during that period, had enough months of sea duty in the Pacific area to have placed my life and limb in jeopardy in war zones on several occasions. The "cushy assignments" of which I speak were the last eighteen months of the war when I was recalled from sea duty and selected for officers candidate school in what was called, at that time, the V-12 program. Shortly before my V-12 class was to graduate and receive commissions as ensigns, and available for general duty assignments, Japan surrendered in August 1945. They only agreed to this surrender after atom bombs had been dropped on Hiroshima and Nagasaki. I had prior experience on amphibious landing craft known as "landing ship tanks," or LSTs, and in all likelihood would have been assigned to LSTs for the invasion of Japan, then in the planning stage. Hundreds of thousands if not millions of casualties would have been suffered in this invasion. An historical development intervened to alter that result.

I realize this next statement is anathema to many people but it's long overdue that we turn away from propaganda and face the truth about this country's history. I have read extensively about that period, along with living through it. An invasion of Japan apparently was the only way to end the war. Japan had declared they would repel an invasion with every man, woman and child in the monarchy. Sixteen million United States servicemen had already been mobilized, four hundred thousand had been killed and two million Japanese had already lost their lives. This slaughter, this war, ended after two bombs were dropped, one on Hiroshima and one on Nagasaki. The loss of life at those two cities, horrific as it was, was less than a land and sea invasion of the Japanese homeland would have been. Most people who criticize the use of these two bombs will not accept the fact that the War would have dragged on longer, with more loss of life on both sides, if they had not been used.

I'll never forget a bumper sticker I saw several years ago, probably on an anniversary of Pearl Harbor. It read, "**If There Hadn't Been a Pearl Harbor, There Wouldn't Have Been a Hiroshima**."

It's easy to defend patriotism with this scenario a background to one's life and difficult to excuse any violation of it.

Another viewpoint that will quickly raise passions is the internment of Japanese civilians in California shortly after World War II began. I believe it was justified. Unless you lived and worked there at that time you have no appreciation for the paranoia that existed in 1942. Japan had attacked Pearl Harbor without warning, killed over twenty-four hundred servicemen, injured another one thousand, and decimated our naval fleet to the extent we had only our aircraft carriers and some small, aging World War I type vessels remaining. This nation was vulnerable to further attacks anywhere including the continental United States and especially the West Coast.

A blackout was in effect up and down the coast. Automobiles crawled along at night with little light to show the road, houses were shuttered and rumors abounded of Japanese submarine sightings just off the West Coast and the imminence of an invasion. We were at war and many believed almost defenseless as a nation. It was in this atmosphere that Japanese living in California were interned. It seemed to be a necessary and prudent action at that time to protect the country against Japanese nationals who may be sympathetic to Japan's cause or planted by design in our coastal ports to relay to Japan the movements of our military ships and personnel. A possible invasion by landing forces was on everyone's mind.

In this context the internment was welcomed by all. In hindsight there is validity to the argument that it may have been premature but in my mind, it was not. In my opinion it was the logical action to take at that time. Criticism of this in recent years has made it sound like this internment was akin to the Nazi imprisonment of Jewish people in concentration camps in Germany. That comparison is ridiculous, and critics who make that assertion know its ridiculous, but do it only to inflame the passions of people who don't know the facts of this period in our history. That's demagoguery at its worst.

Do I know all the facts? No, but I know half of them. I spent most of 1942 in Southern California traveling up and down the coast as a private citizen and as a member of the U.S. Navy. I remember the paranoia of average citizens afraid of an invasion. I remember the stories of enemy submarines just off the coast waiting to relay information of troop embarkations and ship departures and deployments from our ports. And I especially remember the cities and towns under blackout conditions that gave a surrealistic atmosphere to all our surroundings. I believe my firsthand experiences and recollections of the conditions of that time period are equally valid as the history revisionists of today most of whom were not there in 1942. Additionally, neither I nor those history revisionists know what the government knew when they ordered that internment. It's strange that we trust our government for all the services it gives us when we are not at war but as soon as war comes we don't believe anything they tell us.

It's particularly onerous that propaganda of this type flows freely from many of our colleges and universities whose faculty salaries and other expenses are funded in whole or in part by the taxpayers. For some of these schools it's become a mantra of allegiance to the deviant causes they support to distort history in this manner.

Fighting was fierce in World War II as 1942 ended and 1943 began. During this period there were rumors of excessive brutality by

Japanese soldiers to American, British, Australian and Filipino prisoners of war but the governments of these countries would not confirm the reports. They were afraid of even more reprisals by the Japanese if these accounts were published and also sympathetic to the families of prisoners who would hear the details of torture and starvation of their sons and husbands.

But, finally, in 1944 it was decided to release the accounts of several military personnel who had escaped from the Japanese in the Philippines. *Newsweek* Magazine, in February, 1944, in an article headlined "Nation Replies in Grim Fury to Jap Brutality to Prisoners," reported, "America clenched its teeth in rage. With the first impact of the news, the people had shuddered at the story of savage atrocity upon Allied prisoners of war by the Japanese." The article continued, "But most of all the American emotion last week was a fury such as had never before gripped the nation in this war," and summed up the reaction with, "Welling rage among the citizenry sent War Bond sales rocketing; a Bronx woman snapped: 'They're just stinkers.' In Maywood, Ill., and Brainerd, Minn., and Harrodsburg, Ky., many of whose sons had plodded in the Bataan 'march of death,' mothers and wives who had already donated blood and bought bonds and given to the Red Cross, ached to find some new way to strike at the enemy."

Today I find it tiresome that every time someone attempts to have a dialogue on a problem that includes racial factors, that person is quickly branded a racist. Webster's Encyclopedic Unabridged Dictionary of the English Language, 1989 edition, published by Portland House, distributed by Crown Publishers, Inc., defines racism as, "A belief that human races have distinctive characteristics that determine their respective cultures, usually involving the idea that one's own race is superior and has the right to rule others."

No one of rational mind should attempt to deny that races have "distinctive characteristics." Obvious among these are height, color, longevity, susceptibility to medical conditions and numerous other differences. The causation for some of these may go back thousands of years but today, at least, they are relevant and predictable. The second point of this definition is "that one's own race is superior and has the right to rule others." That conviction may qualify labeling a person a racist but not "A belief that human races have distinctive characteristics."

The practice now in this country is to label anyone who doesn't agree one hundred percent with the viewpoint of a minority as racist. That's not challenged or disputed but readily accepted and has ruined many outstanding citizens who have attempted to begin a dialogue on racial issues. These people do not believe their race is "superior," only that races have distinctive (may we say different) characteristics that may or may not impact on the problem or solution under discussion.

It's tragic that such a vital subject as race has been demonized to the point people are afraid to question any assumptions or characteristics surrounding it for fear of being labeled a racist. This negative approach to the subject is obviously a ploy on the part of many minorities who do not want an honest dialogue but prefer instead to have their rationalizations for all minority problems in this country accepted out-of-hand without questioning. And it's not only minorities who practice this deception. They are joined and supported by a large cadre of non-minorities who know this attitude is counter-productive but encourage it nevertheless to gain the support of minority groups.

A more sinister outcome of this demonizing of any topic relating to race, gender, poverty or similar subjects, is the effect it has on free speech. Unless I misconstrue the meaning of the First Amendment to the Constitution of the United States of America free speech is not limited to accepted, popular pronouncements. The objective was the opposite: to give speech NOT popular, NOT universally accepted, free and equal opportunity to be heard.

That has not occurred. Consider the subject of race. A top-level echelon of minorities can (and do so daily) make the most outrageous statements and utter the most outrageous lies about non-minorities but if a non-minority voices the slightest criticism of a minority position, the howl and cry is "racism" or "sexism" or "religious bigot" or whatever fits the demagogue's agenda. It is subsequently demanded the non-minority be banished to oblivion to repent of his sins and, probably, hereinafter, only fit to consort with the Devil.

I don't believe the majority of people in this country realize the degree to which we no longer have "free speech" in the United States. It's rapidly becoming a hollow concept with the tragic consequence we are losing the ability to debate the problems that desperately need solving. The theory of incrementalism has been at play here. Lose a little bit each year and no one objects until one day it's all gone and we wonder where it went.

I'm also reminded of a courageous group of twenty-five or thirty navy veterans of World War II who, just a year or two ago, wanted to bring back an old, rusting LST (Landing Ship Tank) from Greece as a monument in this country of all the sailors and LSTs (over one thousand ships) that performed heroically from the beaches of the Pacific to the landing at Normandy. These men, all in their sixties and seventies now, found this rusting hulk, over three hundred feet in length (the length of a football field), cleaned it up, outfitted it with serviceable gear and equipment from donations, and sailed it, with sub-par navigational equipment across the Atlantic Ocean to Mobile, Alabama to be a lasting reminder of that glorious phase of this country's military endeavors. The United States Coast Guard warned these men not to embark on this trip. They had reservations about the seaworthiness of the ship, its lack of modern equipment and the advanced age of the crew. But these World War II veterans persisted and, despite the odds against them, completed the voyage to Mobile with their skill, their bravery and a patriotism that would not be denied.

Ask these men how they feel about this country and what they did – and still do – to honor and defend it. Ask the other veterans, those who are left, what they think about flag burning and prohibitions against references to God. Better hurry, however. A year ago, a letter circulated by the American Battle Monuments Commission, discussing a lawsuit to prevent construction of a World War II Memorial, stated, "Of the 16 million men and women who served in uniform during the war, the Veterans Administration estimates that only 5 million are alive, and we lose 1,000 each day - over 30,000 a month."

As World War II enveloped the country in 1942 patriotism abounded in every corner, every hamlet. Citizens willingly followed the restrictions of rationing and shortages that affected every aspect of their lives. Women, besides enlisting in all the services, lined up for jobs in factories and shipyards that had never been considered a possibility for their gender. Within months in 1942 the country was producing war material that eventually won the war for us in both the Pacific and in Europe.

Rationing of food began in May, 1942, just five months after war was declared. Other types of rationing began as soon as ration books and stamps could be printed and procedures and offices set up to distribute them. Almost every newspaper and magazine carried an advertisement encouraging people to buy war bonds. Some of their headlines were "Keep Backing the Attack!-WITH WAR BONDS," "There Are More Good Reasons for Buying War Bonds Than for Buying Any Single Thing Ever Offered to the American People," and "Dear Tojo: Herewith I am Returning My Old Silk Stockings."

These ads were unique because the majority were designed and paid for by individual companies, not by the government. In fact, there was one ad that ran in several national magazines that advertised just that phenomena: patriotic, "buy bonds" ads financed by local retail merchants but running nationally where the merchant (advertiser) was probably unknown. It seemed, at times, as if there was almost competition between companies and individuals to promote participation in the war effort in any way possible.

As the war progressed, shortages of all consumer goods proliferated. A survey in January, 1944, in *Newsweek* Magazine, asked "What are some of the shortages which have bothered you (the consumer) the most!" The answers were "elastic tape, bobby pins, washtubs, sheets, women's silk and nylon stockings, infant's and children's underwear and clothing, buckets and pails, metal pot scourers, dress fabrics, pins and needles, alarm clocks, shoes, clothespins, hairpins, electric irons, iron cords, girdles and flashlight batteries." Next interviewers asked, "whether citizens had tried to buy specific items recently and what difference in their lives failing to get these things had made." The answer was, "alarm clocks and elastic tape headed the list of wants causing real inconvenience and hardship. Significantly, the shortage of such heavy goods as electric refrigerators, washing machines, sewing machines, vacuum cleaners and bed springs bothered the consumers least: a sign that the people cheerfully accepted the lack of these durables as 'inevitable in wartime.'"

What a difference from the attitudes of today!

In the decades since the Great Depression the United States has been under continuous assault from much of the world for not sharing all its resources. No matter we have given more assistance in money and material than any other country, to our detractors it's never enough. Many of these nations remain mired in the 15th century with their people in poverty, their women in slavery and their rulers siphoning off billions of dollars of our aid money for their early retirement. And these countries have the temerity to criticize the United States of America!

Here, again, a media critical of any action on the part of the United States that can be in any way defined as aggressiveness, plays a huge, usually harmful, role. I read countless stories in 2002, frequently labeled as "background," reporting on the growing disenchantment of other countries with America's belligerence (in their view). These papers or magazines send a reporter to a country making noises about us terrible Americans and this reporter interviews some men or women "in the street" who have never heard a word about America except that filtered through their government newspaper controlled by that country's dictator. They have no concept of a free press or opposing points of view to any issue.

This "man in the street" is also critical that the United States targets a specific country for the problem despite overwhelming evidence to support our position and then ends up saying "This is all killing our tourism industry. How can we make a living without tourists?" They probably add, "This war (or whatever) might hurt our economy. What will we do to live and feed our families?" The coup de grace of their comment is frequently, "America has too much power. We have none. How can we compete in the world?"

Thank goodness America had the power in World Wars I and II, the Korean War, the Gulf War and several other conflicts where we saved the world.

Their accusations of America's arrogance, intransigence and excessive power are never challenged in these articles. They're merely repeated and allowed to hang out there without refutation. The reader in this country gets a steady diet of this "reporting" and soon he or she accepts it whole cloth. "Gee, those people really hate us, don't they? Why can't we be more accommodating and try to see their side of things." That's the inevitable comment despite the fact we have probably given that country millions or billions of dollars in foreign aid and responded to each of their natural disasters with plane loads of foodstuffs and other material. It's long past time when

Americans should realize we're alternately protecting or propping up most of the world and it's the world's turn to appreciate that instead of showering us at every opportunity with their bitterest vitriolic. This attitude is endemic in our media who feel no war is ever justified, no evil will really come to us, if we just talk nice to them. Their solution, of course, is negotiation. That will solve all problems in their opinion.

The average citizen in the USA can't understand why so much of the world hates us. It's not complicated if you analyze it honestly. There are two primary reasons. One is jealousy of our wealth and liberty, the other our equal opportunity for women. If you or your relatives lived in a country where its policies kept you poverty-stricken and ignorant, wouldn't you be jealous of a country like the United States? Of course you would. These people look at us and our freedom and wealth and can't believe we accomplished all this honestly and fairly. We must have done it by stealing from the rest of the world, ergo, we are to be hated and despised. The example of women is even less complicated. Whether its Asia, Africa, the Middle East, or other areas, a very significant percentage of the countries in the world subjugate women to lowly status and unspeakable discrimination. Any change in that treatment in those countries would bring chaos to their social and religious orders, in fact, it could destroy them. This is an incompatible difference in philosophy and social order that is not likely to be resolved peacefully.

It's differences and jealousies of this magnitude that cause violent conflicts and wars and that is what we are experiencing now. In 1930, without television and other forms of instant communication, these gigantic differences in culture were less visible to countries on the opposite side of the world. Today they are seen frequently, even instantaneously, and the differences are stark and demoralizing for those who live by older, often ancient, traditions.

The United States doesn't owe the world anything. The world owes the United States big-time. No nation has given more lives of its military, fighting FOR the freedom of other countries, than we have. No nation has given more money to support humanitarian causes, and prop up shaky regimes, than we have. No nation has responded to natural disasters, no matter where they have occurred in the world, more generously than we have. No nation has educated more students at its colleges and universities, and then allowed them to return to their homelands to help their countrymen, than we have.

It's worth repeating: The world owes the United States BIG! We don't owe the world ANYTHING.

Given this history and these attitudes it is easy to embrace patriotism and be critical of those who laugh at it. But patriotism is not all black and white. I fear many citizens today who won't burn flags or oppose the Pledge of Allegiance will be lukewarm in their support of an all-out war effort if this country is forced to take that action to once again defend ourselves–and the world–from tyranny or terrorism. That is the danger we face. In a speech given by Tony Snow, FOX News Analyst, on October 15, 2001, at a seminar at Hillsdale College and reported in their publication, *Imprimis*, reprinted by permission from *Imprimis*, the national speech digest of Hillsdale College (www.hillsdale.edu), Snow reports that a major network president, "ordered his charges not to wear flag pins because to do so would constitute 'taking sides' in the war against terror." Snow adds, in this same speech, "(the network president) further embarrassed his company when he told students at Columbia University School of Journalism that his standard of objectivity forbade his rendering judgment on the propriety of flying an occupied jet into the Pentagon" (to blow it up).

William J. Bennett, former Secretary of Education, in an article in the *American Legion Magazine*, May, 2002, reported on a luncheon he had with some leaders in higher education, one of whom near the end of their discussion on teaching patriotism, said, "But do you have to use the word 'patriotism'? It makes many of us uncomfortable."

I'll bet it does!

In the same article Bennett said, "Of the 55 top-ranked universities in the nation, not a single one requires a course in American history, and only three require a course in Western civilization." How sad, how tragic that is.

A shocking comparison of the 1930s to today is evident in our armed forces. Sixteen million men and women were mobilized for World War II. The population of the United States at that time was approximately one hundred and twenty million. That's over **thirteen percent** of the country in the armed forces. Our population in the year 2000 was two hundred and eighty-one million. There were one million four hundred thousand in all the services combined in that same year. That's **one-half of one percent**! I'm certain in subsequent years this figure has increased because of world events but I doubt it has more than doubled to probably one percent. Also, no one has asked the civilian population to "sacrifice." Automobiles continue to roll off the assembly line, television sets become larger, computer and telecommunications gadgets proliferate. In all this crisis who is sacrificing? Only the fathers and mothers, husbands or wives, sons and daughters of those one million four hundred thousand (or more) service personnel. The other two hundred and seventy-five million citizens go on with their lives largely unaffected, many of them largely UNAWARE this country is facing serious threats throughout the world.

Thirteen percent, by the way, of two hundred and eighty million people would be over thirty-six million today (in the armed forces). Any chance of that? Not likely!

Are there lessons to be learned from the Great Depression days? Yes, there are. I leave it to your judgment, however, on whether patriotism remains alive or is only a shell of its former fervor and is there anything we can do to rejuvenate it. I don't believe patriotism can be created or manufactured by design. It must spring spontaneously from the citizenry who realize they are beneficiaries of a unique society and want to protect it. Rosie the Riveter! Where are you when we need you most?

♦ Chapter Eleven: **THE FUTURE**

In the introduction to this book I stated two principles. This country is still young. We have "built our castles in the air," as Henry David Thoreau suggested, but they may need a more secure foundation. The other principle is not to be misled that today's United States is, without challenge, an improvement in all aspects over the United States of past decades, specifically the Great Depression years. We should compare these two periods to see what we can learn from history.

I don't believe there is any doubt we are still foundation building. Two hundred plus years is young in the life of a country. To secure this foundation we need to cement more of the principles of the founding fathers from the Constitution of the United States and not deviate from that document at every opportunity for the sake of convenience. The fact this country has so many voices and resources devoted to tearing it apart as opposed to constructively improving it, is evidence of the shaky foundation. Most obvious is our newfound lack of patriotism which has surfaced so strongly in the last two or three decades. This is a cultural problem and can only be changed if each one of us, and especially our leaders, speak out on it and do so repeatedly. The strident voices of despair and dissension need to be overcome. The deconstructionists have been hard at work. The patriots need to speak up.

We beat our chests about the great diversity of this country. Then the example of a Hollywood, that entertains us with the lowest form of culture possible in television and movies, comes into focus and nary a word of criticism emanates from the media. Pat Sajak, host of the famous *Wheel of Fortune* game show summarized this best when he said of the media, in another speech at Hillsdale College Spring Convocation in April, 2002, and reported in their *Imprimis* publication, reprinted by permission from *Imprimis*, the national speech digest of Hillsdale College (www.hillsdale.edu), "They [the media] think they have diversity in their midst because they take pains to hire a representative mix of gender and race. But there is no diversity of *thought*. On the great social issues of our time, there is an alarmingly monolithic view held by what has become known as the 'media elite.'"

Most important is asking if there are specific characteristics that produce a great society that have been lost in the past seven decades? In writing this book I believe there are. I have tried to be even-handed in applauding many of the advantages we enjoy today: amazingly productive technology, unparalleled in the world, the major advances by women, the potential of television to be a positive influence in everyone's lives, the growing trend to organic foods and the phenomenal increase in Christian-based and home-based schooling with its emphasis on the classics and religion. Overshadowing all of these may be the emergence of the Internet although it is possible we invented a catastrophe there. The problems emanating from the Internet are growing much faster, in my opinion, than the benefits.

In conjunction with these advantages, however, I believe we can learn several lessons from examining history in the 1930s. Most prominent, and probably most important for our future, is the need for huge changes in our educational system. The one we have now is a failure compared to what it could be. Yes, there are schools throughout the country doing an excellent job but in metropolitan areas and many suburbs students are graduating without a basic foundation in reading and writing skills, mathematics and history. Societal concerns have become preeminent in teaching students.

The degradation in colleges and universities is probably the most serious. Countless books have been written recently about the decline and bias in teaching in these schools. You can find a dozen or more at any bookstore. They can't all be wrong. Examples of this influence can always be misleading but sometimes they are useful in highlighting a trend. The number of college professors who tried to justify the terrorist attacks on September 11, 2001, on the World Trade Centers in New York and the Pentagon in Washington are sickening in their intensity and vitriolic tenor. If these opinions are even the tip of the iceberg, and I suspect they are much more than the tip, they are alarming, upsetting and cause for grave concern for the education being given to today's students.

Further indicative of this attitude of any behavior as acceptable, the University of Minnesota Press recently published a book, *Harmful to Minors*, by an author who argues that consensual sex can be healthy for children as young as twelve years of age and not all sexual experiences between youth of that age and adults is harmful. The author said in an interview in the April 3, 2002, Minneapolis *Star Tribune* newspaper, she "supports the age-of-consent law in the Netherlands as a 'good model'– it permits sex between an adult and a person between 12 and 16 if the younger person consents." It was encouraging that the protests and outcry from the public over her book were significant. How many of us can honestly claim we were ready for a sexual "interaction" (as the author terms it) at the age of twelve? It is discouraging that a prominent state university would publish a book of this caliber.

I won't repeat other examples from all the chapters in my book but one or two beg one last emphasis. The decline in musical standards and the terrible lessons that young people today are learning from this music, cry out for change. Some censorship is required. Are we on the road to the approval to cry "fire" in a crowded theater because everyone has a right to do or say anything? I hope not but if some censorship isn't applied to some of this horrible music, it will inculcate too many young people with dangerous messages and set precedents for future deleterious actions.

Of all the contrasts examined in this book the differences in safety, particularly personal safety, are probably the most obvious. Read that chapter again and ponder what we have lost today compared to the 1930s. All the possible answers to this problem, and they are multiple, are not within the length or capability of these pages to answer. But the problem goes to the very heart of the kind of world each and everyone of us wishes for ourselves and our descendants. Realizing and admitting the problem is an important first step but it needs to be corrected to be solved. Civic chaos will be the result if it is not and we continue, as a society, under the mantra of "do whatever makes you feel good" and "the victim is probably to blame."

Given our present reluctance as a society to be judgmental but give tacit approval to any scheme or idea, however onerous and reprehensible, we should heed the words of the English philosopher John Stuart Mill who, in 1859, in his essay *On Liberty*, previously cited in this book, wrote, "The real advantage which truth has consists in this, that when an opinion is true, it may be extinguished once, twice, or many times, but in the course of ages there will generally be found persons to rediscover it, until some one of its reappearances falls on a time when from favorable circumstances it escapes persecution until it has made such head as to withstand all subsequent attempts to suppress it."

Or, to declare it in today's language, "Eventually truth will win out."

Now is the time for us to realistically examine the past and use as a blueprint for the future some of the "favorable circumstances" and some of the "truth" we have forgotten. And ask ourselves, "Do we have the will and the fortitude in this country to make significant changes? For example, at the beginning of the 1990s there were fifteen million people on welfare. Changes to our welfare regulations, emanating from citizens placing pressure on the politicians, provided new regulations and laws that have reduced this welfare total to five million. That's a tremendous achievement. It was done in welfare. Can we do it in other areas equally as critical for change?

Another quote from an author about my age and circumstance is apropos of all I have been writing about in this book. John A. Hutchinson, in 1995, authored a wonderful book titled *Bluejacket*, published by Vantage Press, Inc., 516 W. 34th St., New York, NY., which is a history of his experiences as an enlisted man on several destroyers in the U.S. Navy in the Pacific in World War II, from 1942 to 1945. After detailing countless battles in this epic struggle and the bravery and hardships of the sailors on destroyers, and the successful completion of numerous Navy campaigns and exploits, he writes, on page 568 of this book, "My generation was pretty remarkable, tough and resilient. Before we went off to fight for nearly four years in the Second Great War, we lived through the Great Depression. Without welfare, unemployment checks, or any other government handouts, we survived. Now we see ever increasing numbers feeding at the public trough while hard-working Americans are being taxed beyond all rationality by a rapacious government which has already piled up enough national debt to impoverish our children and grandchildren well into the next century. It is these problems, and many more – including flag-burning, drug-trafficking, illegal immigration, the rewriting of history (before we participants in the events are even dead!), the escalating crime rate, the precipitous decline in morals, the neglect of personal and national responsibility, the denigration of Western civilization and culture – that so sadden my generation. When we returned following the defeat of Nazi Germany and the capitulation of the Japanese Empire, America was the strongest, proudest, fre-est nation in the world's history. We could outfight, outproduce, outinvent, outwork all the rest of the peoples on this earth put together, and we'd just finished proving it. But some fifteen years later, as we entered the 1960s, the generation to follow ours set into motion a decline in the face of America which has continued unabated to this day. And it shows no sign of stopping… With our youngest members now in their mid-sixties, our numbers dwindling down to a precious few, we can only ask again, rhetorically, *'What the hell did we fight the War for?'*"

Those are strident words, but they have the ring of truth, long denied, that John Stuart Mill is talking about in the previous quotation. Why did we fight that War? I have one answer: for the last fifty-eight years of peace! For anyone who served in the Navy in the Pacific area in World War II, *Bluejacket* is a must-read. The above is only a snippet from this marvelous book. It's 628 pages of engrossing reading about the War with Japan in the Pacific. Originally priced at $29.95 it's available now in the online used book market for less. Buy it! Read it!

Does this country have a bright future? Yes, of course. If we face some of our problems honestly. We have many opportunities to grow our greatness. Plant biotechnology, soon to lead us into industrial biotechnology, is still in its infancy compared to its possibilities. We may ultimately be able to replace petrochemicals (from oil) with raw materials from annually renewable agricultural products. Concurrently, the rate of world population growth appears to be slowing. The present total of over six billion people is estimated to grow to only eight billion in the next thirty years. If that sounds ominous, it's far less than the recent growth rate of the population and well within the world's ability to feed with significant improvements in food production occurring each year.

"We need to get out of our easy chairs, love and discipline our children, be involved in our schools, be faithful to the call of God in our lives, be ethical in our businesses, and be involved in our communities." Those are the words of Kay C. James, former State of Virginia Secretary of Health and Human Services and Assistant Secretary for Public Affairs at the U.S. Department of Health and Human Services, in a speech at Hillsdale College in October, 1995, and reported in their February, 1996, issue of *Imprimis*, reprinted by permission from *Imprimis*, the national speech digest of Hillsdale College (www.hillsdale.edu). She went on to say in the same speech, "The village cannot raise a child. Children do not belong to the community. Children belong to the parents who tuck them in at night, wipe away their tears, feed them, and guide them through life."

Kay James thus highlights one of our greatest problems today: The average person is not concerned with our country's future. They look around each day and say to themselves, 'My job is still here, I can make the house payment, my kid is doing okay in school, where should we eat tonight?' That's how far out they're looking!

No better example of this malaise in the general population is our voting record. According to an article by John Balzar in the *Los Angeles Times* in October, 2002, only seventeen percent of the eligible voters exercised their right to vote in the 2002 primaries. But he goes on to suggest the real problem, "the distinction between voting, and voting wisely." Registration has never been simpler," he continues, but "to cast an intelligent ballot requires more than casual exposure to TV commercials." He asks this question: "So, would our democracy be better served if more people voted? As I (he) said, it's not as simple as answering yes."

I believe Mr. Balzar has asked a question of crucial importance to the future of this country. Will - or should – we ever have some level of educational achievement as a requirement for voting? Probably not, but we are going in the wrong direction at the present time to make voting more convenient. Rather than allowing people, often with dubious credentials, to register and vote on the same day, the very least we should have is registration some weeks or months prior to voting. There should also be prohibitions against any political party gathering up people like animals and herding them to the polls on election day to cast a ballot for someone whose name they have never heard. Those voters aren't even robots. They're sheep!

As a corollary to this our biggest danger, other than our educational system, is a prejudicial, biased, monopolistic media. Without honest facts, with slanted news, citizens cannot make decisions in the national interest. There's an abundance of magazines, albeit the attitude is mostly one direction, and more cable TV stations are challenging the heretofore singular viewpoint of the old, established networks. But the increasing number of cities with only one newspaper (one voice, therefore) is dangerous to this country's comprehension and understanding of news and social, economic and political events.

You may remember on the first page of this book I stated I abhor hypocrisy. Logic should prevail in our decisions. If we look at our problems honestly, stop the hypocrisy, we can retain our greatness and go on to even greater heights. The answer is to view our actions in this world on a long-term basis, not a quick fix. The phrase, "It's the economy, stupid," is beguiling to put it delicately. We must make our decisions, we must elect political leaders who act in the interests of what's good for the country overall in the long range. Our economy is only one of our concerns.

My generation suffered through the Great Depression but we persevered. We crawled out of those difficult years, still intact as a society, with our flag, its principles, flying high. There were loud voices in the 1930s proclaiming the advantages of non-democratic political systems. Fortunately they were not listened to except on the periphery of our government. Would we be better off today with a system most other countries are striving mightily to change as they stagger toward some form of democracy? I don't believe we would. But we can't maintain the advantages of the current democratic system unless we are all willing to place the long-term welfare of the United States ahead of our pocketbook when we make our decisions and elect our leaders.

Specifically, we need to cease listening, and trying to pacify, every special interest group that yells and screams about some perceived injustice to which their solution is usually receiving more money from the government (i.e., the taxpayers). A simple rule is applicable here: If people listen to those factions who are continually squawking, they'll keep squawking forever. That's their game plan.

This requirement to understand long-term issues facing the country is becoming increasingly significant as we struggle with threats of terrorism from all over the world. The United States has successfully fought two World Wars. Those of us who remember those Wars, or have studied their history, probably believe this country will never face a bigger threat. That may not be true. The terrorism threat we face today may be "the big one" insofar as war is concerned. Are we ready to face an enemy who fights with weapons of smallpox, anthrax and God knows what else? I hope so, but I'm not overly confident. Some of those biological and chemical weapons could wipe out portions of our population as quickly – or quicker than nuclear devices. A couple of pounds of anthrax released in the air over a major city could infect up to two million people. We are in uncharted territory here. No one knows the answer and that's all the more reason we need to stay strong internally and that means economically, politically, socially and educationally. Yes, especially educationally, so young people can learn from the lessons of history and have ALL the facts on which to make decisions unencumbered by that hideous "political correctness" dogma which has bedeviled us now for decades.

The most lucid explanation of what our foreign policy should be, not only this year but all years, was outlined in a speech by Charles Krauthammer, nationally syndicated journalist for the *Washington Post* Writers Group, on December 4, 2002, at a dinner in Washington, D.C., sponsored by Hillsdale College. The speech is too long to reprint here in its entirety so I will attempt to paraphrase it, with occasional quotations from his talk, as reported in their digest *Imprimis* in January, 2003, reprinted here by permission of *Imprimis*, the national speech digest of Hillsdale College, (www.hillsdale,edu).

The title of the speech was "American Unilateralism." Mr. Krauthammer declares we live in a world that has not existed for at least 1500 years with one country (the United States) so dominant. Its military might is unrivaled and our dominance extends to every other aspect of international life. "We are bestride the world like a colossus. What do we do with our position?" In the face of this opportunity for acting unilaterally why would we want to act multilaterally, such as waiting for approval of the U.N. Security Council before we act, when that's not in our national interest. He says, "My point is not to blame the French or the Russians or the Chinese for acting in their own national interest. That's what nations do. My point is to express wonder at Americans who find it unseemly to act in the name of our own national interest, and who cannot see the logical absurdity of granting moral legitimacy to American action only if it earns the prior approval of others which is granted or withheld on the most cynical grounds of self-interest."

He states we made an extraordinary effort in the Gulf War to not go beyond the U.S. mandate for that conflict. Has that improved the world's view on our good intentions? Obviously not! In fact, we spent the decade of the 1990s acting multilaterally with no plaudits from anyone on the international scene. He continues, "Coalitions are not made by superpowers going begging hat in hand; they are made by asserting a position and inviting others to join," and then adds, "Multilateralism is at root a cover for inaction. Ask yourself why those who are so strenuously opposed to taking action against Iraq are also so strenuously in favor of requiring U.N. support. The reason is that they see the U.N. as a way to stop America in its tracks."

With irrefutable logic he says, "In many parts of the world, a thin line of American GIs is the land mine. The main reason that the U.S. opposed the land mine treaty is that we need them in places like the DMZ in Korea. Sweden and Canada and France do not have to worry about an invasion from North Korea killing thousands of their soldiers. We do. Therefore, as the unipolar power and as the guarantor of peace in places where Swedes do not tread, we need weapons that others do not. Being uniquely situated in the world, we cannot afford the empty platitudes of allies not quite candid enough to admit that they live under the protection of American power. In the end, we have no alternative but to be unilateralist."

He ends his speech, which I have reported too briefly, I'm certain, with this admonition: "We have never faced a greater threat than we do today, living in a world of weapons of mass destruction of unimaginable power. The divide before us, between unilateralism and multilateralism, is at the end of the day a divide between action and inaction. Now is the time for action, unilaterally if necessary."

No one in their right mind wants war. It makes no sense. It's lunacy elevated to insanity. But in the midst of this craziness men and women do heroic things and sometimes lives and nations are saved. It's the ultimate folly of the human race and its brightest hour.

Rather than my words, however, I would like you to heed the words of others, each renowned for their love of country and the principles of right conduct. The first is Margaret Thatcher, former Prime Minister of Great Britain, in a speech to seminar participants at Hillsdale College in February, 2001, reported in their *Imprimis*, reprinted by permission from *Imprimis,* the national speech digest of Hillsdale College (www.hillsdale.edu). She said, "My friends, you're citizens of a wonderful country. You've built the greatest country in the world in terms of establishing the rule of law, defending the freedoms of others, and building a most prosperous future for your people. If those who do not have liberty would be guided by your example, what a much better world it would be. In the meantime, what I call the English speaking peoples, who have for so long defended liberty for the rest of the world, must continue to keep up that reputation, and to help those who still do not enjoy the liberty we take for granted."

The second is the aforementioned William J. Bennett, again from the May, 2002, *The American Legion Magazine*, who quotes a warning to us all from Robert Maynard Hutchins, the late president of the University of Chicago. "The death of democracy is not likely to be an assassination from ambush. It will be a slow extinction from apathy, indifference and undernourishment."

Irrespective of recent developments in terrorism, or the countries that harbor or sponsor it, threats to the United States from our enemies will remain. For this country, the world has changed forever. It will never be the same. We have lost a precious sense of freedom, of liberty, we will not recapture. Our eternal vigilance, preparedness, and, occasionally, military action, will be required from now on. When the face of evil rises in the world, someone must oppose it. Unchecked, it will destroy us all. That's an elementary concept of world-wide affairs that all reasonable people should be able to grasp. Peace at any price isn't peace. It's an invitation to be poked and prodded and stepped on, and eventually slaughtered, when your enemy feels you are vulnerable.

There's also a problem with being a nation that does things honorably. Many nations won't believe or trust us because they wouldn't act honorably under any circumstance.

Lastly, although, regrettably, I have great trepidation quoting the Bible given the antipathy that exists today for religion, one example from that Book is too symbolic to omit. The city of Corinth, in ancient Greece in about 50 B.C., had become a mecca for economic and social activity but this success led to an excess of immorality and depravity including the behavior of many Christians who were prospering there. One technique of the rulers was to promote brutal stadium sports with men pitted against beasts until one or the other was killed or devoured. The objective was to desensitize the populace to other forms of vice and corruption in which the rulers had vested interests.

The Apostle Paul was apprised of this situation and in his first Letter to the Corinthians, 15:33, (Christian Community Bible, Copyright © Bernardo Hurault 1994), wrote, "Do not be deceived; bad theories corrupt good morals. Wake up, and do not sin."

In all humility, if I could paraphrase Paul's admonition, I would say to the current generation, "Do not be misled by the hypocrisy, the immorality, the criminality all around you. They are not new standards. They are new deviations, distractions. Return to the standards in our lives that history shows us are superior to our current practices."

The future of this country – if we have a future – comes to this: There is right and there is wrong. It's not complicated. It's simple. Reasonable people know the difference. If they are the majority, the country will prevail. But there are those who do not know the difference or pretend they don't know. If they prevail, this country is doomed.

ABOUT THE AUTHOR

A.H. Blegen was executive director of the national Association of Data Communications Users, Inc., headquartered in New York, from 1984 to 1992, monthly columnist for *Communications News* Magazine from 1988 to 1992, author of a novel, *A Place With Two Bells*, published in 2002, and a business book, *Records Management Step-by-Step*.

Holds Bachelor of Business Administration degree from the University of Minnesota and lives and works in the Minneapolis/St. Paul area.

Davidson Devendorf Publishing
Brooklyn, New York

The text of this book was set in Cochin.

Manufactured in the United States of America
ISBN-13: 9781494256432
ISBN-10: 1494256436